AF619400

ZERO TO 54

ZERO TO 54

THE MAKING OF A GRATEFUL MIND AND A LIFE OF EARNED PEACE

Joe Sweis

PUBLISHED BY MILE 54 PUBLISHING

www.joesweis.com

Cover design by riverdesignbooks.com

ISBN 979-8-9952318-0-6 (hardcover)

ISBN 979-8-9952318-1-3 (paperback)

First Edition

Printed in the United States of America

To Nathan, Stella, and Zaina.
You are my why.

To Alonzo.

For your unwavering belief.

CONTENTS

INTRODUCTION

This is not your typical gratitude book. I didn't conduct a focus group, obtain a psych degree from an Ivy League school, or spend decades in clinical practice studying the effects of gratitude. This book is hard-earned from the depths of struggle where all that was left in my control were my response and my perspective.

I don't know where you are in your journey, but I know you picked up a book about gratitude and earned peace. That tells me something about you.

Maybe you picked this up because life isn't matching the vision you had for it. Maybe you're successful but an emptiness has you wondering, "Is this it?" Or maybe you're going through a hard time, and hearing someone else's story might help.

I'm not here to tell you what to do; I just want to share my experience. A four-year unraveling of what I'd built, confronting what I'd lost, and a discovery about fulfillment and happiness. Two internal states that so many people chase, thinking they'll find them by going faster. In reality, they're found when we slow down enough to realize that what we're chasing is often right in front of us, but we're just looking right past it. To fully feel them, we need a simple yet profound tool: gratitude.

The common understanding of gratitude is being thankful for the blessings and good in your life. Something happens, you feel euphoric, and you take a few moments to express gratitude for what you've received. That's certainly part of it, but that only scratches the surface.

Gratitude isn't just a reaction to the goodness in life; it's the very tool that reveals it. It's the pathway to discovering what you value most, and to living a more purposeful life. There are levels to gratitude most people haven't even begun to explore.

I started my discovery after one lightbulb moment, in the stillness of an early morning, led me to a 100-day journey of reflecting on gratitude to ground my mind and move forward with optimism despite the uncertainty in my life. It taught me that the most powerful and sustainable growth happens when we bridge grit and gratitude. A combination that forges unshakeable mental strength, guides you toward purpose, and reveals your best life.

I've compiled those 100 reflections for you in this book. Part I shares my story of the breakdown that led me to discovering the power of gratitude. Part II is *your* journey: 100 days of guided introspection designed to help you develop a grateful mind and move closer into a life of alignment.

Lastly, God and my personal faith are an important part of my life, and you'll see that throughout the book. But that's me. No matter your personal belief, this 100-day journey has transformative power. Feel free to replace any references to God or higher powers with whatever reflects your own faith or belief system.

My story provides context.

Your journey provides transformation.

PART I

MY STORY

CHAPTER 1

UNFULFILLED

If a $10 million client walked in right now, I wouldn't care. I wouldn't even try to win his business, I thought to myself. I sat at my desk staring at a color-coded spreadsheet until the dual monitors blurred with CNBC droning in the background. It was another day of portfolio returns, standard deviation, Monte Carlo simulations, and quarterly reviews. I kept thinking about that imaginary client until my gaze drifted to the office door where I played the scene out in my mind.

A heavy click echoes in the office silence as the solid cherry-oak door opens slowly. A faceless man walks in and says, "Hello, I have $10 million in assets, and I'm looking for a new advisor."

"Sure, come on in," I respond in a flat tone with no effort to mask it. The man's demeanor changes as he immediately realizes he walked into a Four Seasons with Motel 6 customer service, desperately searching for a polite reason to walk back out.

That imaginary scene struck a nerve. The guy wasn't real, but my indifference was. This emptiness had been lingering for years, but I'd always buried it with goals and monetary milestones. Whenever the feeling crept up, I'd set a bigger goal or a more distant target, pull out my hammer, and smash through. But this time felt different.

I'd try one more time the only way I knew how, but I'd eventually discover that I didn't need a hammer. I needed a chisel.

•

I'm a first-generation American, son of immigrant parents who came for their American dream. Hard work and entrepreneurism are in my DNA. I washed cars at sixteen, cashiered restaurants and liquor stores, swept garage floors, drove taxicabs in college, and anything else I could do to earn money. I eventually found my way into finance, where I'd spend sixteen years as a financial advisor.

I never thought in a million years I'd end up in finance because I was always a creative person growing up, and I wanted to be an actor or entertainer. As a kid, I remember wanting to connect with people in ways that made them smile. But I forced myself into finance because I wanted to get married, and that meant I needed to earn money in a stable way.

I didn't know much about the financial advisor profession and kind of stumbled into it. The furthest I thought it through was, *If I'm working with money, it'll eventually come my way*. Every profession gets an advantage in their product, so I chose money. Plus, as an advisor, I got to help people, which was true to my nature. That made enough sense in my mind, and I turned out to be pretty good at it.

When I started at the age of twenty-four, I thought earning sixty thousand dollars per year would be all I needed. But years went by barely making ends meet and thickening my skin through rejection and lost prospects. I didn't join a team or have a Rolodex of country club connections from my dad. Just a desk, a phone, and old-school, pound-the-pavement grit. At one point, I was thirty thousand dollars in debt to my broker, but I pushed through the sleepless nights with a relentless pursuit of my vision and an unwavering belief in myself.

It paid off. Every time I hit my target, I raised the bar and set a new one. The sixty thousand I was aiming for became one twenty, which became two fifty, then five hundred, then seven fifty, and then, at age thirty-six, earning more than eight hundred thousand per year, managing $95 million of client assets on a fully discretionary basis, I'd finally won. My typical workweek was thirty to thirty-five hours Monday through Thursday. I was married with three kids, living in one of the most beautiful suburbs of the Bay Area, and my daily ride was a Porsche Panamera Turbo, which I'd occasionally take to the track at Sonoma Raceway. My life was good and hard-earned, so why was I sitting in my office unhappy? Why was my soul screaming, "I'm unfulfilled!" I did everything I was supposed to do.

•

Is this all there is to life? Work, home, kids, 'burbs? It can't be. There's no way I can sit in this chair repeating the same conversations every quarter for the next twenty years.

I went home that day and couldn't shake the feeling. I kept thinking about the Steve Jobs quote, "If today were the last day of my life, would I want to do what I am about to do today?" The answer was a clear no that percolated for months. My biggest struggle was that on paper, a change didn't make any sense. A successful career at thirty-six is about the time you're supposed to enter peak compounding value. Your career is established, you've acquired some assets, and your savings are beginning to multiply exponentially. But my desire to continue growing the business wasn't there, and if you're not growing, you're dying. I knew in the depths of my soul that I needed to make a change. I also knew that as long as I had the safety net of the practice, the raw drive to find my next step would never show up. The only way for me to move forward would be to burn the boats.

I had shared these thoughts and feelings with my wife since that moment of indifference in my office. When I finally decided this was the right move, I said to her, "I don't know what I'm going to do next, but I know that whatever it is means selling my practice. So, I'm starting with that."

I began talking to other advisors and industry connections in search of a trusted successor. It came as no surprise that I raised a few eyebrows:

"You're doing what?"

"Advisors are fighting to get to where you're at, and you're walking away at thirty-six?"

"Are you in a mid-life crisis?"

"Hats off to you, man. I can't imagine doing that."

I'd be lying if I said they didn't cause me to question myself. I lived in one of the most expensive parts of the country as the sole breadwinner with a mortgage and three kids. And let me tell you, kids can't eat love.

But the fear of doing nothing outweighed the risks of moving forward. I just needed careful calculations, precise timing, and enough of a buffer that, should anything fail, I'd have enough runway to pick myself back up.

That single decision sparked what would become one of the greatest transformative journeys of my life.

CHAPTER 2

THE FALL

Transformation is painful. In order to transform into the person who can achieve the goals you set for yourself, parts of you must die. The problem is you don't know which parts, and if you did, you might never have the courage to begin. So, you just go.

That's exactly what I did, every day, for nearly two years following the decision to sell my business. I secured a trusted successor to my practice and set my sights on launching a private equity real estate fund. I pivoted into private real estate because it felt like the entrepreneurial challenge I needed, and the answer to what I thought was missing in my life.

Every weekday started with an alarm at 4:15 a.m. giving me enough time to get my workout in and drop my kids off at school by 8:30 a.m. From there it was some combination of setting up the transition for my practice, building out the real estate fund, poring over hundreds of pages of legal docs for both ventures, consuming everything I could about real estate, attending industry conferences, and running my practice until it sold. And I still managed to make it home for dinner by 5:30.

I felt like a fucking superhero, and I thought that's what crushing it meant. I was chasing my "dream," growing, becoming a new version of myself, and all the other hustle porn[1] mantras. But in reality, I had inadvertently pursued someone else's definition of success. I never slowed down long enough to discover what that signal of emptiness in my office was really about.

Digging it out would require too much work and disruption, and I don't know that I had the infrastructure in my life to do it. So, the path of least resistance was to chalk it up to hitting a plateau in my career. *Why would it be anything else?* I subconsciously asked myself. I did everything I was supposed to do and had everything I was supposed to have. I just needed to level up. This leveling up demanded more of me than I'd ever given. And what I'd eventually learn is that emptiness doesn't stay in one lane. I was trying to solve for it with my career, but I didn't realize how much of my life had been running on the same fault line for years.

That bullshit answer locked me so far into the future that while I was preparing for the next chapter in my career, the distance in my marriage grew further. And what had been silently fraying for years finally ripped in half. The transformation I wanted was about to give me far more than I bargained for. I should've seen it coming. Or maybe I did but chose to ignore it because, like my career, everything was great on paper.

Marriages fail for all sorts of reasons, and I've never really known how to answer the predictable, curious question of "What happened?" How is that a good question? How do you unpack a fifteen-year relationship with hundreds of micro infractions on both sides, mismatched blueprints, build-up, unspoken conversations, loving, growing, failing, good times and bad? You can't. Each party has their own faults and responsibilities as well as their experience in the marriage. So, I just tell people what I tell my kids: "We hurt each other's feelings."

That's the simplest and most honest explanation.

•

1 The glorification of long work hours and being a workaholic.

What the fuck is happening!? I was wide awake at 3:00 a.m. one December night in 2021—a few weeks before our separation became official—lying in my marital bed and listening to the silence of the hour. My wife and I had the difficult conversation that this was the end of the road once we got through the holidays. Like so many years before, on paper everything was still fine, but inside felt very different. My heart was pounding as I looked around my room at what little the moonlight touched. The stillness of the night amplified the thoughts in my head.

Without distractions, my fearful wiring was free to take over as I grappled with the reality that life as I knew it was about to change.

What does divorce say about me? How bad will it be? How do I tell my family? What will my friends say?

My soul knew what was coming, but my mind was scrambling to catch up. Random memories I didn't ask for flooded in and questions came with no order or logic.

Was it that fight? No, we talked about that. What about the argument on vacation a few months after it? That's not it. It's all of it.

Who cares about all that. What about my kids?

I'm not supposed to be divorced. This is something that happens to other people, not me.

This isn't real. We'll figure it out.

At least that's what I tried to tell myself in an attempt to calm down, but I knew it was bullshit.

And my divorce was the kind that no one saw coming. "What?! *They're* getting divorced?" was an annoyance I knew I would have to deal with, but that was the least of my worries. I was more concerned about my kids.

How could I look at them in good conscience, knowing that once we got through this holiday season, the world as they saw it was going to change? The emotional security they knew and relied on was going to cause them to question every other framework in their young lives.

I was spinning with nothing to hold on to. At thirty-seven years old, I was about to lose everything I'd worked the last fourteen years to build—my home, relationships, social life, and identity. I struggled to fully comprehend the magnitude of what was about to happen, but I knew that my life was about to blow up. My heart thumped harder, and in desperation, I went to the one place I've always gone in difficult moments: prayer.

It's funny how, when shit hits the fan, you find your faith real quick. It's by design. Pain and disruption suppress your ego, and you realize how powerless you actually are. But it's in that moment when your ego quiets that something else gets the opportunity to speak. The still small voice inside us all that I've learned to call God. When you listen to it, you make the best decisions, and when you don't, you regret it. But you need to slow down and surrender in order to hear it. Which is exactly what I managed to do.

I was on my side, eyes closed, with my right hand under my head, and a pillow between my knees, hugging the edge of the mattress. My prayers repeated themselves, asking for the same things in different ways, bargaining with God like he hadn't heard me the first time. I eventually ran out of words entirely and didn't know what I was praying for anymore. I was emptied out with nothing left to ask for, and as far inward as I could go.

That's when my mind suddenly fell quiet. All I heard was a brief monologue of words that gripped my core and locked me into a state of sudden calm and awareness.

"It's too late," the still, small voice said. "The ship has set sail, and it's not turning around. But I still love you."

I held my breath for a moment.

What was that?

Where did those words come from?

I didn't know how to make sense of what I just experienced. But I suddenly felt calm. My heart regulated, the questions were gone, and I fell back asleep.

And those words, "But I still love you," would carry me through some of the darkest days to come.

A few weeks later, in January 2022, despite achieving the financial success I'd dedicated my career to pursuing, my wife and I separated, and my family as I knew it was gone.

•

Life began unraveling, right in front of me. My wife and I agreed that she would keep our home, and I would move out. The real estate business wasn't expected to generate much income at first, and the plan, before the divorce, was to rely on personal assets while I grew the business. It was a risk I had carefully calculated, with reliance on the scaffolding around the rest of my life.

But by February, that scaffolding was nowhere to be found, and that plan went out the window. I'd lost three critical pillars of structure in a person's life: partner, home, and financial stability. And the assets I was relying on to carry me would soon be less than half as a result of our divorce. To make matters worse, I also lost about eighty percent of my relationships. Research supports what most men realize the hard way: women tend to be the chief relationship officer in marriages, so when it dissolves, we're left with a pretty thin social network. I'm reminded of the Mike Tyson quote, "Everyone has a plan until they get punched in the face."

In what felt like the blink of an eye, my new reality was life as a single father with shared custody of three amazing little humans, aged 9, 8, and 4, at a time when building out a real estate fund demanded long hours of due diligence, site visits, modeling, investor relations, and quarterly reporting. I was also committed to a two-year consulting agreement for the business I'd sold as part of the purchase contract and compensation agreement. That meant working in a similar capacity as I had before to ensure a smooth transition for my clients and partner.

Becoming a single dad also meant becoming a full-time homemaker, which, for those who don't know, includes 6:00 a.m. breakfast and lunch prep, hustling kids to get them ready and out the door, meltdowns over bumpy socks, cutting my workday at 3:00 p.m. to start pick-ups, afternoon activities, dinner, bedtime routines, and figuring out how to make a house a home. If that wasn't enough, my now co-parent suggested getting our kids a puppy to go between homes with the idea that a cute puppy might offer some comfort during this difficult period. Having never owned a dog before or knowing exactly what it entailed, I agreed. Anything to make it easier for my kids. We got a hypoallergenic dog, but it turned out that my co-parent was allergic to dander, so guess who now had a full-time puppy? Yup, this guy.

In what little spare time I had, I was working through divorce and processing the structural and emotional pain that comes with ending a fifteen-year relationship. The soul-searching and heartache would persist for years, like an undertow that keeps pulling you in as soon as you think you've found your footing.

Lastly, and of utmost importance to me, I was serving as chairman of my church's board as we moved toward ground-breaking on our fellowship hall. It was a commitment I made before my newfound reality. I could've stepped away given my circumstances, but that would've been disruptive to a small church already stretched on volunteers. There was also an emotional component because going through divorce was breaking a sacrament. So, for me, this work was saving grace. I didn't care how much was on my plate. In fact, that's what made it matter more. Anyone can show up when it's easy; it's when things are hard that counts. I promised I would never quit on God because I know He never quits on me, or any of us for that matter.

But life wasn't done pruning me. Several months after our separation, the Federal Reserve began raising interest rates at the fastest pace in modern history and at a magnitude no one could have predicted, which drove real estate into a deep recession. So that new business I was building would soon begin underperforming, and access to capital would eventually dry up.

I was at redline. Each responsibility in and of itself wasn't a problem. It was the summation of all of them that brought me to the edge.

And in the rare moments of catching my breath between perpetual hat switching, I felt a deep ache for the warmth of the home I'd spent years remodeling, gardening, and creating memories in. It was cold moving into a rental with no memories or personal energy.

How do I make this house a home?

I mustered up the courage to walk into HomeGoods on one occasion. I didn't know what that store *was* up to this point in my life. I never had a reason to. But at 1:30 on that Tuesday afternoon, I finally did.

"Yup, this seems like the right place. This is the kind of stuff women buy to make a house feel warm."

The decorative items were staring me right in the face, but I had no clue how to match them together.

Should I get one of the Live Laugh Love signs? I think my kids might like that. What about the Eat Here sign? I know where to eat, why the fuck do I need a sign to tell me? Who buys this stuff?

I paced the store for about forty-five minutes and walked out with some fake plants, a few candles, and a picture of a dog wearing headphones. Baby steps.

But the hardest job of all was soothing my kids. Seeing their world turned upside down caused me the most pain. They never chose to be born, nor did they choose to have the rug pulled out from underneath them. I was holding myself together to be their rock as best I could, though most days I was barely hanging by a thread.

I tried not to let them, or any of the other people I had a responsibility to, see the pressure I was under, but this was next level. I'm pretty sure there were times when the cracks showed. Like the time I nearly broke down at lunch with an investor. He was chewing me out over performance and didn't care about higher interest rates, the Federal Reserve, or the other reasons that were out of anyone's control. I answered his questions, accepted responsibility for what was mine, and delivered the appropriate response despite the swell of emotions in my chest. Maybe he felt it, I'll never know.

My outlets were weekly calls with my life coach, working out, my brother, a few close friends, and the occasional bout of dysregulated screaming when no one was around. I was brought to tears more in that first year than my lifetime combined. And at times, sat broken at the bottom of my stairs, begging God for help and doubting the wisdom that you never get more than you can handle. It was in these moments that I gripped those words…

"But I still love you."

CHAPTER 3

FOLSOM 54

One December morning, while my kids were with their mom, I got to the gym for my 5:00 a.m. workout—thirty minutes of cardio followed by seventy-five minutes of weights and stretching. After twenty-six years my routine is like clockwork. My body goes on autopilot, and for two hours, my mind roams wherever it needs to. People sometimes ask if I'm training for something. I joke and say "life," but that was no longer a joke. My life had become a full-contact sport, and I had to have strength and conditioning. It's also my favorite release valve. But for some reason, that morning, nothing was working.

This is too fucking slow.

Every rotating step of the stair mill at level thirteen felt like an eternity, and I didn't have the patience for a thirty-minute slow burn. I switched to the stationary bike, thinking speed would help, but it left my upper body neglected. I went back to the stair mill for a second chance but got off just as fast as I got on. Both felt like half-ass workouts, and I couldn't decide which half was better.

I needed something visceral. Something to channel the pressure that had been building all year. I wasted fifteen minutes bouncing back and forth before the voice of reason finally emerged.

You look like an idiot, Joe. Either commit to one machine or skip cardio.

Fair point, skip it is. Time was precious and I needed to settle into my workout before losing the morning. I grabbed my water bottle and started toward the weight room the same way I had a million times before. But this morning, when I walked by the treadmills, something about them caught my attention. I don't know what it was or why, but I stopped dead in my tracks, looked to my left at a row of them and thought, *Fuck it, why not?*

Mind you, I had never been a runner. Ever. I'm 5'11" and 205 lbs. of muscle with pancake-flat feet. I'd been a meathead for so long I forgot there was a thing called running shoes. Probably why I thought it would be okay to get on a treadmill wearing Nike Metcons, which are weightlifting shoes with minimal flexibility. Ignorance is bliss, I suppose. Still, I stepped on, hit the green button, and started running. I ran fast enough to get the demons out, but at a pace I could maintain.

Within minutes, I hit my stride and found that autopilot state I was so familiar with. The movement felt natural and allowed my mind to run faster than my feet. Raw emotion processed with every step. Frustration, anger, sadness, regret, fear, grit—all of it. It felt like I hit the release valve on a pressure cooker that had been simmering for hours. By the nine-minute mark, my endorphins were in full effect, and I was tapping the up arrow into a full sprint.

The belt whizzed as I pushed my lungs to maximum capacity with every compression. I finally found the visceral outlet I'd been looking for. I held that pace until the 'elapsed time' read '10 minutes,' tapped the 2 mph button, and powered down to a walk.

Holy shit; that was it!

I got off the treadmill feeling clear and reenergized. And with my heart rate higher than usual, I was able to take my weight workout up a notch.

Over the next month, I ran a handful of times, like a prescription, and I even got a pair of running shoes. It was proving to be a viable outlet, and ten to fifteen minutes seemed to be all I needed.

Running gave me something else I hadn't felt in months: control. Everything else in my life felt like it was happening *to* me, but running was something *I chose*. My results were tied directly to my efforts. If I wanted one more minute, I pushed for one more minute. Every time I stacked one of those little wins, I proved to myself that I could handle more than I thought I could.

•

I sat on my couch one night ruminating on the chaos in my life and wondered if it would end or if this life of perpetual grind was my new normal. *What if it is? What if I should've kept my mouth shut, sitting in my office staring at the door?* I knew the answer. In that case, I'd be in a different kind of fucked up. A guilt for feeling unfulfilled despite the blessings in my life.

What a shitty predicament. I did what I was supposed to do and was left feeling empty. I decided to change and pursue something more meaningful, and now my life was fucked. It felt like every decision I made was destined to blow up in my face and life was laughing. I started to get angry. But that anger turned into fuel. If life was going to be hard, it was going to be hard on *my* terms. That was about the moment I decided to do something harder than all of my responsibilities combined.

I'm gonna run an ultramarathon.

Not a marathon, or a half, or a 10k. Nope, I'm going full-blown psycho run. For those who don't know, an ultramarathon is any distance longer than 26.2 miles.

It was bold, but I didn't overthink it. It just felt like what I needed to do at the time. I looked for upcoming races nearby that seemed reasonable on paper, and one in particular jumped out at me. It was a new trail race in its second year, only two hours away, no altitude, and it took place on a weekend that I didn't have my kids. Perfect.

Not knowing anything about distance running, I signed up to run Folsom 54—a 54-mile ultra with more than 7,000 feet of vertical climb on the trails around Folsom Lake, California—with only ten weeks to prepare.

A lot happened during those ten weeks, but only one story matters for this book. Twelve days before the race, I went out to the actual course for my last long run. I had never run a marathon before, let alone a proper trail, and I wanted to see if I could at least complete *that* distance.

I quickly learned that not all miles are equal. My first trail experience exposed what it meant to run over rocks, technical terrain, and single-track paths that at times could barely fit one foot. I felt the athletic joy of running downhill with my mind moving faster than my feet, calculating every next critical step that would keep my momentum and spare me from tripping and smashing my face.

This dance with the mountain was fun and exhilarating, but slowly beating away at my body as the hours went by. Running turned into walking and running, which became walking and jogging, and then just walking. But by mile 21, I could barely even do that because everything hurt. A deep aching soreness throbbed from my hip flexors, through my quads, and down to my calves. My legs felt like concrete and my feet like they had been beaten with a mallet. My hips were in excruciatingly sharp pain that hit with every step because being flat-footed alters your biomechanics. Flat feet compromise your shock absorption and impact the lower kinetic chain, resulting in a lot of stress on your joints and hips. I didn't know this at the time.

My mind started racing with fear and doubt. Anxiety began to set in because not only had I signed up to do something ridiculous, but I also announced my run publicly alongside an effort to raise money for a cause I care deeply about. Because that's what people do when they do these things.

Anxiety turned into full-blown panic. I forgot about the pain in my legs because I was now battling my thoughts.

What the fuck were you thinking signing up for a 54-mile run and announcing it? You can't even make it to marathon distance!

No problem, I'll just postpone and pick another race. People will understand.

What about the people who donated to your fundraiser?

It's a donation. The money still went to a good cause. I'm sure they won't care. And I'm still going to run, just not this one.

Well, what about your kids? Are you going to model even more quitting to them? And why the fuck did you pick this rocky-ass, single-track trail? No way anybody runs this stuff! Why didn't you pick a flat road race?

The voice of reason emerged again. *It ain't the fuckin' trail, Joe! If you were out running on a road, you'd be bitching about how hard the pavement is thinking you should've run the trails.*

So what is it? Why are you out here?

I was standing still, drenched in sweat, hunched over like a basketball player with my hands on my knees, staring at my shoes. The silence of the mountain and the question in my head suspended time. My heartbeat and breath began to slow.

Why are you doing this?

No answer.

Why?

Still no answer.

Why the fuck are you doing this?!

A soft whisper came out, "Because I can."

My mind went silent.

Because I have the legs and bones to carry me.

Because I have the strength to endure. And for that I'm grateful. I'm grateful I can even attempt something like this.

In that moment, I felt a deep and enduring appreciation for my physical health. I felt gratitude to my core.

My son was born with osteogenesis imperfecta, a brittle bone condition. We learn so much from our children, and his spirit and strength when facing challenges taught me not to take my health for granted. That's why my gratitude hit so deeply.

Finishing this ultra with minimal preparation was also going to be my opportunity to model to him, and to my daughters, that it's mental strength that gets you to the finish line. Strength they already have, but I knew seeing it from their father would reinforce that they have everything they need. They became my why.

With those deep feelings of genuine gratitude, I felt the tension in my legs lighten and started walking again. My pace picked up, and I ran the next 3 miles thinking about nothing but the things I'm grateful for in my life. I still only made it to 24 miles that day because it was getting dark, I didn't have a headlamp, and the battery on my phone was about to die. Not to mention I was out of water. But on that run, I scraped the surface of gratitude's power.

On race day, May 6, 2023, for the majority of thirteen hours in the rain and mud, my focus was on gratitude for everything and everyone in my life: from my kids to the workers who made my shoes, and anything else I could possibly think of. I literally touched every single course marker and said, "Thank you to whoever marked my path." I thanked every single volunteer at the aid stations for their time and support. That focus and energy are what empowered me to finish despite minimal training. Despite the fact that by mile 48, my right leg had completely locked up, and I was struggling to even limp on it. Tylenol and Advil weren't working. Stretching wasn't working. Nothing but a positive mind fueled by gratitude that had already made the decision to finish. The immense pain of running 54 miles with my build at 39 years old didn't matter.

At 54.9 miles I finally saw the words "Finish line this way," with an arrow pointing to the right. It felt like mile 1 again, and I was sprinting. Around the bend, off the trail, and down the stairs that led to the parking lot where the finish line was. I heard the cowbell ringing and saw my babies waiting for me. I embraced them with hugs and kisses. They are the best part of my life. We held hands and crossed the finish line together. It was all worth it. It was one of the most magical experiences of my life.

I did it. I did it. I fucking did it!

Euphoria flooded me. The post-run chills, the cold sweat on my shirt, the pain in my feet, busted toes, aching hips, and throbbing quads added substance to my victory. Challenges and struggles are what make the story great. I came to understand that gratitude isn't just for the good in our life. It's for the hardship that strengthens and develops us. For the resistance that guides us. It's the tool that reframes your mind and uplifts your energy regardless of your circumstances.

That was the birth of Zero to 54, and it wasn't about the miles. It was about taking on challenges, doing what you said you were going to do, and moving forward with gratitude.

The euphoria lasted about a week before reality settled back in. And it would be two more years before I fully discovered what gratitude unlocked in me. Two more years of baptism by fire, tears, relentless responsibility as a single father of three, plus a few more ultras—including a 63-miler in the Lost Sierra Mountains with 11,500 feet of vertical climb that took me 17 hours to finish.

4/23/2023

my long run

Today I went up to Folsom lake to sample the course and it was one of the top 5 to 10 experiences of my life!

I didn't realize just how different trail miles are from road miles even though I'd run a few times on lime ridge. In total I ran 24 mi with 3,120 ft of total elevation gain! Apparently I went in severely under prepared. I had my two liter camelbak, water bottle, and fuel (gel packets, sandwich etc.). Around mile 11, I started to run out of water and asked a few people for water which they gave me. About 1 mile later I found a running stream followed by a man made well. At mile 13 I turned back around to get to my truck. Then at mile 21 the dialogue started in my head. Doubt started to creep in as did panic. What happened then was magic. I remembered why I was doing this. Thought about Nathan, and the example I'm setting for him. And I started to fill myself with gratitude. I was grateful for the girl that poured me water. I was grateful for the guy

⟹

that gave me the remainder of his water bottle. I was grateful for the running stream. I was grateful for the people that built the well. And on and on I filled myself with gratitude. My legs started to numb and I just ran the last 3 miles. Then, as the sun started to set, I found the nearest parking lot and these two ladies were kind enough to give me a ride back to my car. It was such a magnificent experience to truly learn the power of gratitude

My journal entry from the long run before Folsom 54.

Crossing the finish line at Folsom 54 on May 6, 2023.

CHAPTER 4

TWIN HUNDREDS

I sat in the early silence one January morning in 2025, absorbed in the pink and purple streaks through the window as the sun began to rise. My thoughts roamed a mental Sahara in a blank gaze, the one where your eyes fixate—you're looking at something but you're not really seeing it. My eyes eventually locked with my dog, who accompanies me during my morning reflections. I stared at him and wondered what he might be thinking. He stared back, probably wondering the same thing. Both of us suspended in time with no direction.

I had satisfied my commitment to my business partner, and I completed my term as chairman of my church's board. I also signed up to run my first 100-miler: The Leadville Trail 100 Run, a 100-mile ultra in Leadville, Colorado.

On paper, it looked like progress. Obligations fulfilled, my load a little lighter, and I was growing as a runner, which was my new favorite outlet. But the bigger obstacles of rebuilding those three critical pillars I'd lost—partner, home, and financial stability—still remained. Most important of which was the business.

Real estate was still in a recession, and the pain of delivering bad news to investors for consecutive years weighed heavily on me. They didn't care that the Federal Reserve had raised rates at an unprecedented pace and obliterated the market. I was the manager and had to accept all that came with the territory.

What good is practicing mental toughness on the trails if you don't practice it in your daily life? Especially when growing the business was uncertain, I didn't know my next step, and it was now a race against time before my bank account dried up. I started to feel as though stability would never return to my life no matter how many times I got back up.

The frustration and emotional fatigue were taking their toll, like the miles on the mountain, slowly beating away. It was when I paused to look at how far I'd come that I'd ask, "When will I ever catch my fucking break?"

And the voices of grit would immediately answer, "You don't catch breaks, Joe; you fucking make them."

"Right," I'd whisper back with a sigh. "But I am human."

As I wrote in my journal that morning and reflected on the path forward, I noted the emotional whiplash of great days followed by stretches of feeling lost. It was exhausting, and I was tired of the highs and lows.

There has to be a better way, I thought.

Not from hope or a change in circumstances. But something foundational and so deeply rooted that nothing external could move it. It had to come from within.

That's when I realized that response and perspective are all we truly have control over. I can't control if the Federal Reserve raises or lowers interest rates, change the fact that I'm a single father and lost half my time with my kids, or that being one drastically changes your social dynamics and compounds the effort required to achieve your goals. I am "the man in the arena," and I can't control what adversary comes through the gates or if the crowd boos or cheers. All I can control is how I respond and what I allow these things to mean to me.

Reining in the highs and lows and getting control of my mind would be critical to rebuilding my life, taking it to the next level, and executing under the now-added pressure of time. I snapped out of my gaze and picked up my phone to open Instagram for some inspiration.

Hustle porn, hustle porn, ad, running, dad jokes, healing, hustle porn for running, ad, positivity, healing and positivity...

Lightbulb.

Where's the gratitude? Why are people barely talking about it? What if I could add it to the conversation?

Not the fluffy cognitive gratitude, but the deep, enduring kind for joys and challenges alike.

That Zero to 54 kind of gratitude as a tool.

That lightbulb also made me realize I had only practiced morning gratitude sporadically since that first ultra. If I could run fifty-four miles fueling my mind with gratitude, then it could definitely give me the foundational shift I needed. I mean, the caffeinated gel packets, PB&Js, and electrolytes definitely helped, but the point stands. It's the strong mind that crosses the finish line. Given the task ahead, and what I discovered during Folsom 54, it was time to armor my mind with it and share it.

I committed to start every morning by reflecting on gratitude and listing ten things I'm grateful for. I also decided to post those reflections on Instagram, for a couple of reasons: first, to hold myself accountable by creating a public streak of consecutive dates that I wasn't allowed to break; second, it would become my way of adding gratitude to the conversation. I would emphasize gratitude irrespective of challenges, and my life had no shortage of fuel.

On January 27, 2025, I wrote my first post. I continued to post no matter how I felt, where I was, or what was happening in my life. I made the decision, and that was it. There were plenty of days I didn't want to practice gratitude or didn't even feel particularly grateful. But I practiced anyway, even if it felt empty. Because that's what persistence looks like. That's what it takes to develop a habit and achieve your goals. Especially on the mornings when I was flat out frustrated with the process of rebuilding my life:

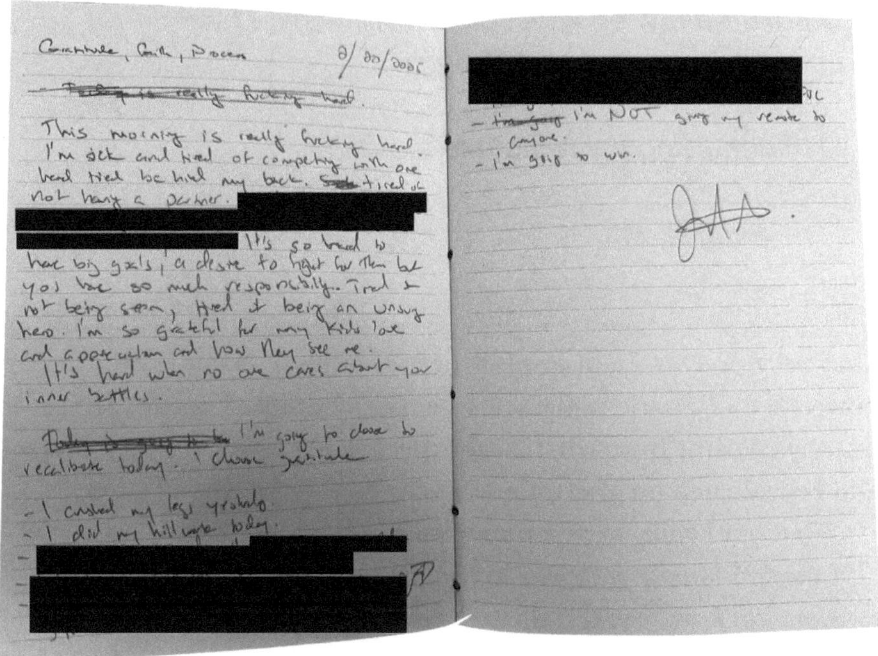
Gratitude, Faith, Process 2/20/2025

This morning is really fucking hard. I'm sick and tired of competing with one hand tied behind my back. tired of not having a partner.

It's so hard to have big goals, a desire to fight for them but you have so much responsibility. Tired of not being seen, tired of being an unsung hero. I'm so grateful for my kids love and appreciation and how they see me. It's hard when no one cares about your inner battles.

I'm going to choose to recalibrate today. I choose gratitude.

- I crushed my legs yesterday.
- I did my hill work today.

- I'm NOT giving my remote to anyone.
- I'm going to win.

Journal Entry: February 20, 2025

Gratitude, Faith, & Process.

This morning is really fucking hard. I'm sick and tired of competing with one hand tied behind my back. Tired of not having a partner. It's so hard to have big goals, a desire to fight for them, but you have so much responsibility. Tired of not being seen. Tired of being an unsung hero. I'm so grateful for my kids' love and appreciation and how they see me. It's hard when no one cares about your inner battles.

But I'm going to choose to recalibrate today. I choose gratitude.

I crushed my leg day. I did my hill work. I had productive calls and meetings.

I'm not giving my remote to anyone.

I'm going to win.

That became Day 25 of the journal: "Gratitude is your mind's most powerful tool. Sharpen it. Use it." I wrote it because I needed to hear it. Every post came from what I was experiencing on that given morning, and I ruminated on gratitude incessantly.

What am I going to post tomorrow?

How can I apply gratitude to inspiration and a growth mindset?

How can I apply gratitude to the challenges I'm facing?

How can I connect ideas and concepts that are seemingly independent, to gratitude?

Random thoughts led to deeper realizations, and reflections began to compound. Most mornings I'd find myself in a stream of awareness thinking of the different ways gratitude could be applied in my life.

By day 100, I felt I had said all there was to say about gratitude at the time, and 100 sounded like a nice round number to end at. What I didn't realize, though, is that those hundred days were the apex of my transformation. Gratitude became a baseline of stability no matter what I faced, including the realization that my business wasn't going to move forward the way I needed it to.

Every opportunity and potential partnership to grow and expand fell through. I went toe-to-toe with some top-notch real estate firms competing for executive talent that managed portfolios in the billions of dollars. My little company against Goliaths. I even opened dialogue with a prominent hedge fund to discuss potential collaboration. They all loved my grit and what I was able to build as an outsider. But each time, they opted for the more secure path.

"Sorry Joe, but I took an offer at a firm that checked all my boxes. They've been around for twenty years."

"As much as I love what you're about, and I know you'll do well, I need to go with a more established company."

"A start-up in this market carries too much risk. It's a long road that doesn't make a lot of sense to walk right now. Let's keep in touch."

As frustrating as it was, I knew they were right. I picked a hard business to start at what turned out to be the worst time possible. I had to take inventory and accept that my business was going to be in a holding pattern for the time being.

Outside of work, I ran three ultramarathons (including a 52-miler with plantar fasciitis) as part of my training for the Leadville Trail 100 Run, started building a podcast, and unknowingly laid the foundation for this book through my daily posts.

But most important of all, I found a state of inner peace I'd never experienced. Stress and anxiety decreased meaningfully despite the uncertainty in my life. I no longer felt defeated or overwhelmed by my challenges. Instead, I felt supported by them. I viewed them as a parent practicing tough love, seeking to bring out my best.

I began to realize that my lack of fulfillment that sparked this whole journey was an absence of purpose and awareness, not the job itself. It was during these hundred days of immense gratitude focus that I finally let go and stopped chasing what I thought mattered, to slow down and begin noticing what actually does.

I began to fully experience the "little" wins happening every day, which were actually big wins and privileges: notes from my kids, the excitement on their faces when I'd pick them up from school, watching them do their best in sports, listening to my son play the drums, watching my daughters dance and create art, and the opportunities to teach them valuable life lessons. I found more joy in spending time with my family, catching up with friends, noticing kind gestures from strangers, and taking inventory of the countless ways I am blessed in my life despite the challenges my mind is wired to focus on.

I found deep and enduring peace.

Toward the end of the hundred days, I noticed something else that stopped me dead in my tracks. My list of ten gratitudes transformed from thoughtful observations into a varied repetition of the most substantial and meaningful parts of my life: my faith, my kids, my health, my family and relationships, joys and challenges alike, and other forms of support I received on those days. The goals of feeding my ego and amassing material possessions I thought mattered began to diminish. Gratitude revealed what I value most in life and reoriented me toward it. I developed what I call "a grateful mind." A way to see the truth about life that is often staring you right in the face.

Practicing daily gratitude regardless of your circumstances helps you see reality as it truly is, not as you think it is or ought to be. It also has the power to introduce you to your true self by refocusing the mind on what it values most. The Zero to 54 journey emphasizes gratitude for the challenges in life because, I believe, they exist to develop and guide us.

That lesson, one of the most pivotal for me on this journey, cemented itself on July 20, 2025. Less than a month before my 100-mile run in Leadville, Colorado, I walked into my doctor's office to receive a stem cell injection for my posterior tibial tendinitis. A condition that felt like a knife through my arch if I attempted even the lightest run. My tendon had a micro-tear with some pretty bad inflammation as a result of overtraining.

He explained it would be highly unlikely that I'd heal in time, let alone be able to run 100 miles. "It's not worth permanent injury, Joe. This isn't your career," he wisely told me.

Someone must have called my ego because I went straight into denial. *You can give that advice to someone else,* I thought.

I had trained all year for that race, and it meant so much to me. Days of running when I didn't feel like it, running at 5:00 a.m. or in 105-degree heat, forcing it into my busy schedule, and balancing my personal goals with responsibilities. Distance running is incredibly difficult for me, which is why I set out to do it in the first place.

Leadville was going to be proof, to my kids and myself, that I don't have quit in me. Running was also the one area of my life where there were no sales, no waiting on a response, and no external parties involved. It was me versus me every time. I had the illusion of full control and refused to accept that this too could be taken away. Nothing was going to stop me.

"Okay," God and His universe said. "We'll see about that."

The next day I was back on the bike. Instead of resting my foot, I was worried about losing my conditioning. If I couldn't run, I'd bike. If I couldn't bike, I'd swim. I was not taking no for an answer and would rather try and fail than never try at all.

About a week later, I got a call from my mom. We talk all the time, so her calling wasn't unusual. But for some reason, as soon as I saw the caller ID I knew something was off. I felt it. Then I heard it in her voice before she even finished.

"Something happened to my back, and I'm in a lot of pain. I've been in bed for two days. I'm sorry Joey, but I don't think I can make it to Colorado with you."

"No, don't worry about it. What happened? Are you okay?" Of course, my immediate response was to be there for her, but this meant I had no help with my kids. My siblings had obligations in their lives, and my co-parent had already made travel plans. So even if my ego wanted to take the risk of running on a busted tendon, I now had no one to watch my kids while I was out running for an entire day or more. It was the final nail in the coffin, and the race was taken away.

A sense of loss bathed me.

My business isn't moving forward, I'm battling as a single father of three kids every other week, I refuse to adjust my goals because of that, and now I can't even do the one thing that brought me so much freedom and joy. The one area of my life I thought I had control over. Why? Why can't anything go my way?

It hurt to have the race taken away. It's one thing to lose because of your mistakes, it's another when it's factors outside of your control. Something that was becoming all too common in my life. Deep sadness is the only way I can describe it. It fucking sucked.

Having a grateful mind doesn't mean always being cheerful. We're human, and it's important to acknowledge all of our emotions. Especially the ones that require grace.

I packed away my vest, trekking poles, and running gear. I wasn't getting back on the trails anytime soon and didn't want to be reminded. I wanted to forget about the whole damn thing. But one question kept circling my mind in the week that followed.

Where's the gratitude in this?

Practice what you preach, Joe. Day 73, no matter what happens and no matter how hard, find gratitude, right?

Days went by with no answer. Maybe there wasn't gratitude to be found in this one. Maybe it was just shit luck. Nothing more, nothing less. Train smarter next time, and have a back-up plan.

That's definitely one takeaway. But there had to be more. I can't explain every little breakthrough moment I've experienced over these years, but I knew there was a reason. I refused to stop asking why.

And then it hit me.

Stopped at a red light on my way home, sulking in the reality that nothing seems to be working for me. A huge sigh of relief finally came out.

That's why!

That damn race owned me.

It had to be taken away in order for me to see that I already ran the race that mattered! I proved I don't quit and didn't need a 100-mile trail to do it. I smiled ear to ear, and just as fast as the light turned green, gratitude shifted my perspective.

In the four years since my journey began, I successfully managed my business through one of the worst real estate recessions in modern history. I delivered to my partner, who bought my practice, by ensuring a smooth transition and keeping client attrition to a minimum. My church's fellowship hall has been completed, and it's magnificent! All three of my kids are getting As in school with a few scattered Bs, and they're thriving socially. We've created some amazing memories together, and our house is filled with photos that aren't from HomeGoods. I even trained the dog to walk off-leash and taught him a few tricks. Biscuit has been a wonderful addition to my family. Despite the chaos, emotional turmoil, and unfathomable difficulty throughout my journey, I honored *all* of my commitments.

Gratitude didn't make my life better; it made *me* better. It armored my mind through my darkest days, empowered me to live more purposefully, and pointed me in the right direction.

If you recall, this journey started with me getting everything I thought mattered, while losing what actually did. It finished with losing what I thought mattered, but finding what actually does.

Part II of this book is my 100 daily reflections that transformed my relationship with life and helped me develop a grateful mind. Each day opens with a prompt and a reflection I wrote during that season, followed by space for your ten gratitudes and your own reflection. It was never my intention to turn them into a journal when I wrote them, but it's turned out to be a journey worth sharing. The reflections are mine. The practice is yours.

The world is missing the depth of gratitude's transformative power. We all have an inherent need to run our mountains. We need grit because it's what we're built for, but we also need our humanity—our spark and connection. In completing this journey, I hope you experience the power of gratitude in your life.

Gratitude is medicine.

P.S. As I was writing this, I realized that my 100th day of gratitude landed on the same date as my first ultra that taught me gratitude: May 6. That's also my daughter's birthday. There's no way I could've planned that. I just kept taking the next step until life aligned.

PART II

YOUR JOURNEY

FROM MY JOURNEY TO YOURS

Everything you just read wasn't theory. It was my life. Divorce, losing my home, building a new business in a recession, single father, ultras, and serving my church. It was a four-year crucible where every part of my identity was stripped away.

In the middle of that, I realized grit wasn't enough. I could push through almost anything, but I couldn't think my way into peace. That's when I committed to what I could control: my perspective. For 100 straight days, I trained my mind to become grateful no matter what was happening.

The pages you're about to work through are not generic prompts. They are the exact reflections I wrote to myself during that season. The same thoughts I used to push through business rejection, show up for my kids, and keep running ultras when nothing on paper was getting easier—including money.

They are how I became unshakeable.

This 100-day journey is the method to build your own unshakeable foundation. If you show up every day, especially on the days you don't feel like it, you will not relate to your life the same way on Day 100 as you do today. But in order to complete the journey, you need the right mindset.

A GRATEFUL MIND

Before you begin your 100 days, I want to share what I learned about gratitude because understanding what it is and what it isn't will change how you experience the practice.

My experience taught me that gratitude is a tool to reframe your perspective, shape your experiences, and rewire your mind. I discovered this organically through pain, not by studying the science. I also found a difference between experiencing grateful moments and having a grateful mind.

Grateful moments are fleeting reactions to positive feelings that acknowledge the good in one's life. *A grateful mind*, though, is one where gratitude is the default wiring that sees all life experiences, pleasant or not, as happening *for* you, not *to* you. It intentionally expresses gratitude, regardless of life's circumstances, for joys and challenges alike.

I've learned that challenges—distinct from tragedies and loss of life—don't exist to hold us back, but to develop and guide us toward the goals we set for ourselves. In that sense, you chose your challenges when you set your goals. I'm not saying blame yourself for any hardship you might be experiencing; I'm encouraging you to look at it through a different lens.

If you want to build a business, you'll face the challenges of capital, finding customers, and running operations. If you want to build a meaningful intimate relationship, you'll be challenged to balance time and navigate human experiences. If you want to trail run, you're going to struggle with cardio, strength, and endurance. Challenges are a form of support in your life because they help transform you into the person who can achieve the goals you set for yourself. And for that, they deserve an expression of gratitude.

The moment you express gratitude for the challenge itself is the moment the pain begins to ease.

But expressing gratitude doesn't come naturally. It's a choice that takes effort, and in the face of hardship, needs to be forged through perseverance and grit. Earned peace requires consistent daily practice and can't be taken away once you have it, though it can be lost if you stop.

WHAT GRATITUDE IS NOT

Gratitude is not a tool that magically changes your circumstances. You're not going to suddenly love your difficult boss, find fireworks in your relationship, or laugh in the face of adversity. It's a tool to change your perspective, and that's important because perspective shapes reality. The objective is, with consistent practice over time, to begin to see your circumstances differently and change your relationship with them. You'll see challenges as a parent practicing tough love, seeking to bring out your best. Changing that relationship refocuses your mind and uplifts your energy. It shortens the duration of stress and opens the door to positive change no matter what's happening around you.

The question isn't whether gratitude works; it's whether you're willing to practice it when life is most difficult. Because real change comes in ways you'd never expect.

THE ZERO TO 54 MINDSET

BEYOND GRATITUDE

"It wasn't about the miles. It was about taking on challenges, doing what you said you were going to do, and moving forward with gratitude."

The journey you're about to embark on is the complete Zero to 54 experience. It's taking on a challenge of 100 days of daily gratitude and showing up every morning, even when you don't feel like it. It's doing what you said you were going to do and moving forward with gratitude.

I didn't realize it was the complete experience until I wrote this book. Yes, gratitude was the tool I used to excavate the truth about my life and remind myself of who I am. Yes, it's a daily practice. And yes, I used the structure of a journal. But gratitude alone isn't what brought about the most profound changes in me. It's in combination with the other two—taking on challenges and doing what I said I was going to do—that gratitude ultimately revealed what was already in front of me. Those three pillars are what brought my life into alignment.

Most people spend their lives pursuing happiness, fulfillment, and peace through achievement, accumulation, and external validation. They grind. They perform. They build their lives and arrive at the destination only to feel a sense of emptiness. What society calls a "mid-life crisis."

That doesn't mean abandon ambition or pretend money and achievement don't matter. Of course they do. Porsches are fun cars! Want everything your heart desires and pursue it relentlessly. But know *why* you're pursuing it. A Porsche because you love cars and earned it? Aligned. A Porsche to peacock in front of your friends? Misaligned. Same car. Different wiring. Alignment is when goals are chosen from your authentic self rather than being inherited from the world around you. One feeds you. The other drains you no matter how many times you win.

On the other hand, what if Porsches aren't even on your radar? What if you're just surviving (as I was for four years)? You're getting through the day, handling responsibilities, without feeling any pull at all. That's a different kind of misalignment.

The problem is nobody chooses misalignment. You inherit it from an early age. Over the years, who you are gets buried beneath every signal of modern life that points outward—title, status, and possessions. The person who follows those signals arrives at the destination feeling empty because they lost themselves along the way. And if you don't know who you are, how can you choose the right direction?

I stumbled on all this not by design, but by never quitting. I chose the wrong direction because I followed the wrong signals. When I decided to correct course, life painfully stripped away every false one. I had to keep moving forward until I reconciled all of it and discovered what matters most to me. That's the experience I want to share with you. And you don't need the wreckage to benefit from the outcome.

The flywheel of challenges, commitment, and gratitude will reveal who you are, and keep you in alignment with that person. The challenges in your life reflect your aim. Honoring your word is what gets you through them. And gratitude grounds you in your truth, which in turn sharpens your aim. That's how the flywheel spins. A grateful mind is the cornerstone that holds it all together.

That's why the goal of Part II is to help you establish that. It requires the discipline of consistently writing what you're grateful for, long enough for the patterns of what you value most to emerge. The struggle most people will face isn't finding things to be grateful for; it's believing that their daily lives are worthy of gratitude.

So when you ask yourself, "What should I list?" you're effectively asking, "What's worthy of my gratitude?" The ego wants big wins and breakthrough moments. Those are important, but they're the summation of small daily gifts and hard challenges. If you can't find gratitude in the little wins, the big ones will never feed your soul.

When you realize that all gifts received—from the struggle to the sunrise—are worthy of gratitude, the list becomes easier. You stop judging your life and fully experience what's already in front of you.

This is what you'll discover over 100 days. That's how you earn your peace.

HOW TO USE THE JOURNAL

For one hundred consecutive mornings, read the daily prompt, then take a few moments to reflect and connect with the ways it applies to your life. Use the "Reflections" page to write your thoughts and how you might apply them throughout the day.

Writing is powerful because it forces you to articulate your thoughts. That provides clarity, gets them out of your head, and brings them to life. When you're done writing your reflections, sign your name at the bottom. Your signature symbolizes ownership and your commitment to 100 days.

After signing, list ten things you're grateful for in your life. **You must write ten every day.** Three to five come easily, but ten is where the power of gratitude reveals itself because it forces you to slow down and take inventory of your life.

You will likely struggle to get to ten at first, and that's the point. To see the beauty that already exists in your life, you need to slow down. If you find yourself repeating items, that's okay, but be sure to add *why* to avoid mechanical gratitude.

That said, throughout your journey, there will be times when gratitude *does* feel mechanical or empty. It's normal to have those days. Write it down anyway. This isn't about manufactured positivity or pretending everything in life is okay. It's about training your mind to find solid ground even when life feels unstable.

Some days you won't want to practice. You might even find it stupid or pointless, and that's where grit comes in.

Transformation doesn't happen on the days you feel grateful; it happens on the days you don't but practice anyway.

UNDERSTANDING THE PHASES

Phase I – Laying the Foundation	**15 days**
Phase II – Into the Struggle	**54 days**
Phase III – Mastery	**31 days**

Phase I *is very basic.* The goal isn't breakthroughs; it's orientation toward gratitude. Starting any journey requires covering the basics and building the habit. Don't judge the experience by this phase. Just get through it.

Phase II is grueling. It's repetition, thought, reflections, questioning, and plenty of opportunities to quit. Don't. This is literally where all the heavy internal lifting is done. Gratitude will reveal itself, but you won't see it until you look back. Repetition is what rewires.

Phase III is cementing the practice and introducing you to more advanced concepts of gratitude. This is an exciting phase filled with breakthroughs because you will have learned so much about yourself.

These reflections were written during one of the most difficult periods of my life. There are a lot of recurring themes around challenges, which reflect what I was experiencing at that time.

You'll also notice the daily prompts gain more substance over the 100 days. That's because gratitude reveals its power through consistent practice over time.

I encourage you to develop a routine that's repeatable for the full 100 days. Maybe set an alarm fifteen minutes earlier, journal with your morning coffee, add it to an existing habit, or just find a quiet time and place for reflection each day. Whatever it is, make sure it's repeatable.

It's important to not miss more than one day. If you have the discipline to never miss a day, you'll feel an amazing sense of achievement at the end. In reality, life happens and people are going to miss a day here and there—I get it. But don't miss more than one. Once you miss more than one, you invite the opportunity to miss more than two, and then it's game over. Your mind will start justifying relentlessly. Keep your rhythm. It's a priority like brushing your teeth.

THEME INDEX

While the journal is designed to be completed in sequence, I'm aware that every journey is different, and some days you might need to look for inspiration that meets you where you are, not where I was. This book was written in the trenches—use it as you see fit. If you complete the days out of order, that works, but be sure to complete all of them, and save day 100 for the last day.

Gratitude for Challenges and Struggles

Reflections on hardship, grit, growth, and transforming adversity through gratitude.

Days: 10, 15, 17, 18, 25, 27, 30, 33, 35, 37, 40, 46, 47, 48, 57, 59, 62, 63, 66, 67, 68, 69, 73, 77, 79, 85, 86, 87, 89, 90, 91, 95

Gratitude as a Tool for Presence, Peace, and Inner Calm

Reflections that foster acceptance, mindfulness, and inner alignment.

Days: 1, 2, 6, 7, 8, 11, 13, 14, 16, 19, 20, 21, 22, 24, 28, 29, 32, 34, 36, 39, 43, 49, 50, 51, 52, 56, 58, 64, 65, 66, 71, 80, 92, 93, 94, 99

Gratitude for Daily Blessings and Things Taken for Granted

Reflections that highlight the overlooked gifts, comforts, and constants in our lives.

Days: 3, 4, 5, 23, 41, 42, 44, 53, 54, 55, 60, 61, 78, 84, 98

Gratitude and Relationships

Reflections centered on people, connection, and expressing appreciation to others.

Days: 12, 45, 53, 60, 72, 82, 88

Uncategorized Reflections

These reflections don't fit neatly into one theme but offer value in their own right. They can serve as motivational check-ins, to process insights, or as lightbulb moments.

Days: 9, 26, 31, 38, 70, 74, 75, 76, 81, 82, 83, 96, 97

PHASE ONE

LAYING THE FOUNDATION

Day 1

Feed your mind gratitude every morning.

Writing 10 things you're grateful for in your life first thing upon waking sets your energy for the day, because that's when your mind is most malleable. It brings you to the present, reminds you of your abundance, and sets your thoughts on a positive trajectory for the day.

The first week is about establishing a baseline and getting into a rhythm. Take a moment now to reflect on the blessings in your life. Write down whatever you feel on the Reflections page, then make your gratitude list for the day.

I'm Grateful For:

1. ______________________
2. ______________________
3. ______________________
4. ______________________
5. ______________________
6. ______________________
7. ______________________
8. ______________________
9. ______________________
10. ______________________

Reflections

_/_/_

Signature: ________________

Day 2

Gratitude is lean protein for your mind.

Why is morning the critical time to practice gratitude? Just like a lean protein shake is a great way to ignite your metabolism with something clean upon waking, feeding your mind gratitude ignites your day with positive energy. It orients your thoughts in your blessings and frames your mind toward abundance. It's the optimal mental launchpad for the day.

The goal of today is to bring awareness to the benefit of practicing gratitude in the morning. No deep profound aha moments just yet. We're establishing a baseline. Write down whatever is on your mind and list your ten gratitudes.

I'm Grateful For:

1. ____________________
2. ____________________
3. ____________________
4. ____________________
5. ____________________
6. ____________________
7. ____________________
8. ____________________
9. ____________________
10. ____________________

Reflections

_/_/_

Signature: __________________

Day 3

Sometimes it's hard to find gratitude beyond the basics. Keep digging. That's the benefit.

Starting gratitude is usually easy—my health, my family, my house, my car, my clothes, etc. That's when we start to ask, "What else?" That question helps unlock the power of gratitude. Start getting granular. What else?

I'm Grateful For:

1. ______________________
2. ______________________
3. ______________________
4. ______________________
5. ______________________
6. ______________________
7. ______________________
8. ______________________
9. ______________________
10. ______________________

Reflections

_/_/_

Signature: ________________

Day 4

So many things are taken for granted that shouldn't be.

Take inventory of things and people in your life, how much do you take for granted? Your shoes, your clothes, your relationships, your music and entertainment, technology, the roads and infrastructure you use every day, and so on. Think of your local coffee shop or favorite lunch spot. Someone took a risk to open that business, deals with the administrative hassles of running it, and likely poured their life savings into it. And all you need to do is show up and order.

There's plenty to be grateful for when we slow down to reflect. What's the daily, ever-present support in your life that you might be taking for granted?

I'm Grateful For:

1. ______________________
2. ______________________
3. ______________________
4. ______________________
5. ______________________
6. ______________________
7. ______________________
8. ______________________
9. ______________________
10. ______________________

Reflections

_/_/_

Signature: ________________

Day 5

Focus on what's abundant, receive more of it. Gratitude is the tool.

It's easy to focus on what's missing, we all do it. The deal that hasn't closed, the text that never came, or the version of life we thought we'd be living by now. Lack is loud, and it stems from our fearful wiring. Abundance, on the other hand, is quiet. It's the breath you take for granted, the friend who always shows up, the roof over your head, the food on your plate. Focusing on the abundance and positivity in life will attract more because you can't fuel positivity with negative energy.

Is there an area of your life you might be fueling with negative energy?

I'm Grateful For:

1. ____________________ 6. ____________________

2. ____________________ 7. ____________________

3. ____________________ 8. ____________________

4. ____________________ 9. ____________________

5. ____________________ 10. ____________________

Reflections

_/_/_

Signature: __________________

Day 6

Gratitude is a positive sum game. Play it.

There is literally no downside to practicing gratitude. It uplifts your energy and radiates to those around you. It attracts more blessings into your life because it empowers you to show up as your best self. In that state, you're more productive, helpful, and attractive to those around you. It takes a few minutes of slowing down and reflecting but stays with you the rest of your day. It's such a high return on investment of your time so why *wouldn't* you invest in it?

What's an area of your life where you could show up better if you expressed gratitude for it? Said differently, where are you withholding gratitude?

I'm Grateful For:

1. ______________________ 6. ______________________

2. ______________________ 7. ______________________

3. ______________________ 8. ______________________

4. ______________________ 9. ______________________

5. ______________________ 10. ______________________

Reflections

__/__/__

Signature: __________________

Day 7

Gratitude is the antidote to negativity.

Keep focus on what you have, not on what you don't. If you're feeling down, it's likely because you're focused on what isn't working in your life. If you're trying to progress while thinking about what's not working, you'll operate from fear, make mistakes, and create chaos. Gratitude and negativity can't coexist.

Practicing gratitude during a hard time is no different than lighting a candle in a dark room. It's a starting point to find your way out. Start with what *is* working in your life and what blessings you *do* have. Where do you need to light your candle today?

I'm Grateful For:

1. ______________________ 6. ______________________

2. ______________________ 7. ______________________

3. ______________________ 8. ______________________

4. ______________________ 9. ______________________

5. ______________________ 10. ______________________

Reflections

_/_/_

Signature: ________________

Day 8

Gratitude → Presence → Peace

Gratitude humbles us to focus on the blessings we have in this moment, irrespective of circumstances. Being in the present moment leads to peace because we're not dwelling on the past or anticipating the future, regardless of whether those thoughts are positive or negative.

Do you feel like you're ruminating on the past or waiting on the future? Where would you direct your energy if you could only focus on this day? What wins do you want to visualize for *today*?

I'm Grateful For:

1. ______________________________ 6. ______________________________

2. ______________________________ 7. ______________________________

3. ______________________________ 8. ______________________________

4. ______________________________ 9. ______________________________

5. ______________________________ 10. ______________________________

Reflections

_/_/_

Signature: ________________

Day 9

It's okay to practice "empty" gratitude. Those days still contribute to a constant state.

List your gratitude even if you don't really feel it; it happens in all areas of life. Sometimes you don't feel like going to work, or the gym, or certain special occasions, but you still do, and that matters. Gratitude is the same. Recall the times you didn't feel like doing something but did it anyway and how glad you were that you did.

How do you feel when you push through discomfort to do what needs to be done versus when you don't? How can you use those feelings to reveal the best version of yourself—the version that honors your commitments, no matter your circumstances?

I'm Grateful For:

1. ______________________
2. ______________________
3. ______________________
4. ______________________
5. ______________________
6. ______________________
7. ______________________
8. ______________________
9. ______________________
10. ______________________

Reflections

__/__/__

Signature: ________________

AID STATION #1

During an ultramarathon, there are aid stations throughout the race to support runners. This 100-day journey, like an ultramarathon, is supported by aid stations every ten days.

By now, you might be experiencing:

- Resistance or difficulty developing the habit.
- Gratitude that feels mechanical.
- Struggling to get to ten and being forced to slow down.
- Prompts that feel very basic.

That's all by design. When I started my 100-day journey, I didn't have a regular gratitude practice. I started with the basics and that's what's reflected. That's the start of *any* journey or new habit.

The resistance and foreign feelings are normal. The next ten days will land better, and you'll start to develop a rhythm if you stick with it. And if you need help, accountability is very powerful.

I posted on Instagram for accountability. You can do the same if you want with the hashtag #zeroto54, or, if it's more comfortable, let a friend know. Tell them you've embarked on a 100-day gratitude journey and to expect a text from you every ten days.

Now get going. Just focus on the next ten days.

"A journey of a thousand miles begins with a single step."
Laozi

Day 10

Challenges are what make the story great. Be grateful for them.

We know, in theory, what we need to do when going through a difficult season, but when we're in the depths of it, hope can sometimes be hard. It's often not *what* we hear, but *how* we hear it that keeps us moving forward. That's why you'll find various iterations of the same theme as you progress through the 100 days. Today, remember that your story wouldn't be great if you didn't have challenges to overcome. It's not happening *to* you, but *for* you. It's giving you substance.

How are your challenges shaping your story, and what would it be like to have gratitude for them instead of fighting them?

I'm Grateful For:

1. ______________________
2. ______________________
3. ______________________
4. ______________________
5. ______________________
6. ______________________
7. ______________________
8. ______________________
9. ______________________
10. ______________________

Reflections

_/_/_

Signature: ____________________

Day 11

Gratitude changes perspective. Perspective shapes your reality.

How we see things determines how we experience them. If we pause to hold gratitude for the good we take for granted *and* the struggles we fail to appreciate, we experience life differently. That opens doors that wouldn't otherwise be open because we're moving with positivity.

At this point, you might begin to notice and embrace the idea that you can be grateful for both joys and challenges. What's a challenge or dispute in your life that, if you slowed down, you could find gratitude for the opportunities it's creating?

I'm Grateful For:

1. ______________________
2. ______________________
3. ______________________
4. ______________________
5. ______________________
6. ______________________
7. ______________________
8. ______________________
9. ______________________
10. ______________________

Reflections

__/__/__

Signature: ____________________

Day 12

Polish your loved ones with gratitude.

Gratitude helps polish people we love, allowing us to see them whole. Gratitude isn't just for the experiences and material things in our lives, but for our relationships as well.

Whether it's your friends, spouse, or family, over time we can take them for granted. If we slow down to "polish" and express gratitude for the ways in which they show up, it deepens our appreciation for them and strengthens the bond. Relationships are what matter most in life, just ask anyone on their deathbed.

Who in your life can you surprise today by expressing gratitude for the things they consistently do for you? Call or text them.

I'm Grateful For:

1. ______________________________ 6. ______________________________

2. ______________________________ 7. ______________________________

3. ______________________________ 8. ______________________________

4. ______________________________ 9. ______________________________

5. ______________________________ 10. ______________________________

Reflections

__/__/__

Signature: ____________________

Day 13

Gratitude isn't always easy. Medicine doesn't always taste good.

Expressing gratitude during a difficult time can be tough. It takes humility and mental strength to be grateful when life isn't going your way. By expressing gratitude for what you already have, you nurture a more positive outlook (even if just a little), and eventually you'll drown out the negative. What hardship will you find gratitude in today?

I'm Grateful For:

1. ____________________	6. ____________________
2. ____________________	7. ____________________
3. ____________________	8. ____________________
4. ____________________	9. ____________________
5. ____________________	10. ____________________

Reflections

_/_/_

Signature: ____________________

Day 14

Gratitude doesn't come naturally. It's a habit you must choose to develop.

Nature didn't wire us for gratitude; it wired us to hunt and survive. Gratitude is a habit that requires development through consistent effort and awareness of the things we take for granted. Develop the mindset, shift your perspective, and you will begin to notice new opportunities. Keep pushing, especially when it feels difficult.

If you're struggling to reflect, try writing about what you want to accomplish today. Even if it's just one thing to anticipate, with gratitude, for the opportunities it can bring.

I'm Grateful For:

1. ______________________
2. ______________________
3. ______________________
4. ______________________
5. ______________________
6. ______________________
7. ______________________
8. ______________________
9. ______________________
10. ______________________

Reflections

__/__/__

Signature: ____________________

Day 15

It's not supposed to be smooth all the time, otherwise you'd slide all over the place. Be grateful for the friction.

Think for a moment: if everything in your life worked out the way you wanted, and nothing went wrong or challenged you, would you really enjoy that? Life's friction—those annoying setbacks, tough days, or endless climbs—are what give you grip to move forward. Without them, you'd never build strength.

Today, name one piece of friction in your life. A tough conversation or a missed goal, for example, that you can thank for making you wiser and stronger.

I'm Grateful For:

1. ______________________
2. ______________________
3. ______________________
4. ______________________
5. ______________________
6. ______________________
7. ______________________
8. ______________________
9. ______________________
10. ______________________

Reflections

__/__/__

Signature: ________________

PHASE TWO

INTO THE STRUGGLE

ENDURING THE LONG ROAD

(54 DAYS)

By now, the novelty of daily gratitude might be wearing off. You might be wondering, "Where's the benefit?" "This is starting to feel a little redundant." "I'm not that much happier," or "Things haven't really changed." It's important that you stick with it because this is when habit formation starts to take hold. If you're already realizing a benefit, that's awesome. If not, be patient. Change is coming.

The first two weeks you laid the foundation and explored the basic aspects of gratitude: the habit, nourishment, things we take for granted, attraction, reframing, relationships, and acknowledging difficulty. There will be many days ahead that don't feel productive, and you might feel like quitting or skipping a day. Don't.

Don't skip, don't quit. Keep going. Nothing happens in linear fashion. Look at the stock market, it's always peaks and troughs. The people who experienced linear value were invested with Bernie Madoff. You don't want that.

Day 16

Gratitude anchors your mind in your blessings and the present.

When the demands of life become too much, the weight on your shoulders too heavy, and it feels like nothing is working, how do you respond? Everyone answers that question differently, but one thing is certain: if you respond from a negative space, it won't be good.

A grateful mind doesn't eliminate hard days or challenges. It's a tool that anchors your mind to the blessings and support you have, which leads to being more present. Any time you're feeling down about a situation, frustrated, or even angry, pause and list ten gratitudes. If you can't find ten, start imagining life without your current blessings. You'll notice an instant energy shift.

I'm Grateful For:

1. ______________________________ 6. ______________________________

2. ______________________________ 7. ______________________________

3. ______________________________ 8. ______________________________

4. ______________________________ 9. ______________________________

5. ______________________________ 10. ______________________________

Reflections

_/_/_

Signature: ________________

Day 17

The high road is exhausting because it's uphill, but it leads to the top. Be grateful for opportunities to walk it.

When you're dealing with drama, it's easy to want to react emotionally because that feels good in the moment. But any time we react (rather than respond) with a negative emotion, we give away our power to something outside of us; we allow that thing or person to change our behavior. Taking the high road is hard, but all good things are, and that's how we grow.

Is there a situation in your life where taking the high road will make you a better person? Can you reflect on the opportunity for growth with gratitude?

I'm Grateful For:

1. ______________________________
2. ______________________________
3. ______________________________
4. ______________________________
5. ______________________________
6. ______________________________
7. ______________________________
8. ______________________________
9. ______________________________
10. ______________________________

Reflections

_/_/_

Signature: ________________

Day 18

Let it go with faith and gratitude.

It sucks when things don't happen the way you want or expect. Have faith that something else opened up, and be grateful it did.

Experience has taught me that a closed door is a bullet dodged. Letting go isn't giving up; it's trusting that God has your back and something better for you. Gratitude eases the process by centering your thoughts on what you've gained and dangers you've potentially avoided rather than what you've "lost."

Is there a door that's closed on you where you can lean into faith and gratitude that it happened for your benefit?

I'm Grateful For:

1. ______________________
2. ______________________
3. ______________________
4. ______________________
5. ______________________
6. ______________________
7. ______________________
8. ______________________
9. ______________________
10. ______________________

Reflections

__/__/__

Signature: ________________

Day 19

If you can't be grateful for the little wins, how can you be grateful for the big ones?

When going through transformation or looking for happiness, it's easy to experience destination addiction, the story in our heads that says, "I'll be happy when I get [insert whatever you want]." That discounts the blessings and wins right in front of us. The problem is even if we arrive at our destination, it feels empty or short-lived because there was no fulfillment attributed to the process. We arrived from a place of lack. Imagine a team that was bitter after every win until the championship. Would they be fun to watch?

Where are you on your journey? What are the little wins you need to celebrate or remind yourself of? Who else benefited from those wins? Is nineteen days of gratitude a win? I think so.

I'm Grateful For:

1. ______________________
2. ______________________
3. ______________________
4. ______________________
5. ______________________
6. ______________________
7. ______________________
8. ______________________
9. ______________________
10. ______________________

Reflections

__/__/__

Signature: ____________

AID STATION #2

By now, the prompts are landing differently than they did in Week 1.

- They're starting to go deeper.
- Your understanding of gratitude is broadening.
- You might be internalizing the concept of gratitude for challenges.
- It's shifting from a list to a lens.

Pay attention to any rushing. Life is competing for your attention: work, family, travel, friends, the unexpected disruption, all of it. The temptation is to check the box and move on. Don't. The whole purpose is to slow down long enough to notice and feel the life already in front of you rather than the one you're chasing.

If you're struggling to prioritize, good. You're shifting your habits and patterns, and that's uncomfortable. Push through.

One last thing. Remember that gratitude doesn't eliminate challenges—it changes your approach to them. You can hold space for both grief and gratitude. You can acknowledge that life is difficult while being aware of the gifts you receive daily.

Text your friend or share on your media and move on. Get through ten more days. #zeroto54

"There's so much beauty in the pain of this thing. I appreciate the really really tough times as much as I appreciate the great times. And it's important to go through that progression, 'cause I think that's where you really learn about the self."

Kobe Bryant

Day 20

Leave the past where it belongs. Be grateful for the experience.

Attachment to past experiences can impair the present. How? Attachment to negative experiences will cause fearful responses while attachment to positive ones leaves you trying to recreate. Let them go. Enjoy today.

What can you let go of today that's been holding you back? Toss it in the ocean. Tie it to a hot air balloon. Swipe up on it. Whatever you need to do, let it go.

I'm Grateful For:

1. ______________________
2. ______________________
3. ______________________
4. ______________________
5. ______________________
6. ______________________
7. ______________________
8. ______________________
9. ______________________
10. ______________________

Reflections

_/_/_

Signature: ________________

Day 21

Sincere gratitude reduces down days.

By sincere gratitude I mean deeply felt appreciation rather than the cognitive or mechanical kind. That doesn't mean there aren't moments of processing bad news, getting upset, or having a frustrating day. But a grateful mind limits the time you spend in that headspace. Gratitude requires humility, awareness, presence, and a focus on abundance, which shortens the duration of stress.

If you're going through any kind of transformation, you've likely experienced stretches of great days followed by not-so-great days. A consistent written gratitude practice can smooth out that volatility. What have you observed about your energy over the last three weeks?

I'm Grateful For:

1. ______________________
2. ______________________
3. ______________________
4. ______________________
5. ______________________
6. ______________________
7. ______________________
8. ______________________
9. ______________________
10. ______________________

Reflections

_/_/_

Signature: ________________

Day 22

Faith + Gratitude is unshakeable.

Faith that what's yours is coming and gratitude for what you already have is an unshakeable combo. When you're in the shit and it's hard to have faith (whether it's based in your religious beliefs or your capacity for trust and conviction), find gratitude for the blessings in your life. When it feels like your abundance isn't growing or that you're not where you want to be, have faith that more is coming. Life is unfolding for you, as it's supposed to, as long as you keep moving forward.

Learning to bounce between faith and gratitude can make a huge difference. What area of your life feels like it's not enough or that you're not where you want to be? What would your energy feel like if you were certain more is coming? What would it look like to have that energy with what you already have?

I'm Grateful For:

1. ______________________
2. ______________________
3. ______________________
4. ______________________
5. ______________________
6. ______________________
7. ______________________
8. ______________________
9. ______________________
10. ______________________

Reflections

__/__/__

Signature: ________________

Day 23

Imagine your life without the things you take for granted.

I lived in Jordan for six years growing up, and it was such an eye-opening experience. We once had an Iraqi refugee family visit us for a day. At the end of the day, I learned something I would never forget: the children were ecstatic just being in a house with modern furniture and comforts. I was twelve and remember thinking, *The same couches I sit on to complain about my life, they sat on and found joy.* That was probably my first lesson in gratitude.

Maybe you can't move to a developing country but imagine if someone with less stepped into your life. What would they experience? Maybe you could volunteer somewhere and step into someone else's life. How might your perspective of the things you take for granted change?

I'm Grateful For:

1. ______________________ 6. ______________________

2. ______________________ 7. ______________________

3. ______________________ 8. ______________________

4. ______________________ 9. ______________________

5. ______________________ 10. ______________________

Reflections

_/_/_

Signature: ________________

Day 24

The goal is a state of gratitude, not just moments.

A consistent gratitude practice rewires your baseline. It heightens your awareness to the blessings of life's gifts so that they, both large and small, are fully experienced. That doesn't mean life is rainbows and unicorns 24-7, it means valuing and appreciating the blessings in your life regardless of circumstances. That keeps you in the present moment and preserves your peace.

What negative thoughts have you been dwelling on? Now name three gifts you received this week that you overlooked. Flip the attention.

I'm Grateful For:

1. ______________________________ 6. ______________________________

2. ______________________________ 7. ______________________________

3. ______________________________ 8. ______________________________

4. ______________________________ 9. ______________________________

5. ______________________________ 10. ______________________________

Reflections

_/_/_

Signature: ________________

Day 25

Gratitude is your mind's most powerful tool. Sharpen it. Use it.

There are many mental tools at our disposal: patience, growth mindset, framing, critical thinking, and so on. But gratitude, in my opinion, is the most powerful and most versatile. It can be used in most situations, improves happiness and relationships, reduces stress, and lightens difficult circumstances. Most importantly, it keeps your mind anchored in truth, the present, and what's working for you.

The benefits are endless, so keep your gratitude sharp by using it. What challenge are you facing right now? List three ways it's making you stronger. Then say "thank you for giving me the opportunity to [grow/learn/become stronger]." That's gratitude in action.

I'm Grateful For:

1. ____________________
2. ____________________
3. ____________________
4. ____________________
5. ____________________
6. ____________________
7. ____________________
8. ____________________
9. ____________________
10. ____________________

Reflections

_/_/_

Signature: __________________

Day 26

The universe can't use you in a negative state. You're benched. Gratitude and positivity empower you to give and receive.

We're all interconnected, and God uses each of our gifts and talents for good and to help others. Being in a negative state is like being on injured reserve: your gifts and talents exist, but they're not usable. It's hard to give and receive fully. If you're in a tough place, that's okay—it's part of the process.

Gratitude is a powerful tool to return to a positive state of mind and get back in your game. It's not overnight; it happens through consistent, daily practice. Are you on the bench or in the game? Wherever you are, list gratitude for the support that's powering you forward.

I'm Grateful For:

1. ______________________________ 6. ______________________________

2. ______________________________ 7. ______________________________

3. ______________________________ 8. ______________________________

4. ______________________________ 9. ______________________________

5. ______________________________ 10. ______________________________

Reflections

_/_/_

Signature: ____________________

Day 27

If you're focused on what's lacking, how do you perform?

If you're focused on abundance, how do you perform?

It's easy to get caught up in what's lacking. Maybe you're not running as far or as fast as you want, or you're not in the kind of shape you'd like to be. Maybe your business isn't humming, or a relationship (with someone or yourself) is struggling. If that's your focus, your energy and performance will suck. Period.

If you're focused on the miles you *can* run, the habits you *are* changing, the customers and business you *do* have, and the parts of the relationship that *are* great with gratitude, you'll perform better. Today, reflect on what *is* going right.

I'm Grateful For:

1. __________	6. __________
2. __________	7. __________
3. __________	8. __________
4. __________	9. __________
5. __________	10. __________

Reflections

_/_/_

Signature: ________________

Day 28

Gratitude takes you from the fearful future to the peaceful present.

When we dwell on the future, it's typically some derivative of control, which stems from fear of not getting the outcome we want. Let's take the opposite approach: say you're excited and anticipating something good. Well, now you've created an expectation, and expectations are a precursor to unhappiness. You've put yourself in a lose-lose situation.

Staying present is hard to practice but far more enjoyable. Do you find yourself living in the future or past too often? Observe the patterns. When you're done, express gratitude for the progress toward your future goals and the lessons and experiences the past has given you. In doing that, you acknowledge the future and past without dwelling in either.

I'm Grateful For:

1. ______________________________
2. ______________________________
3. ______________________________
4. ______________________________
5. ______________________________
6. ______________________________
7. ______________________________
8. ______________________________
9. ______________________________
10. ______________________________

Reflections

__/__/__

Signature: ________________

Day 29

Gratitude isn't just for what's in your life, but for yourself.

Rapper Snoop Dogg gave one of the greatest acknowledgements in his Hollywood Star speech when he said, "Last but not least I wanna thank me." And that's really important. Express gratitude for your mindset, your ability to work hard, and your awareness to embark on this journey. You are the common denominator of the good you have created in your life.

Be aware, this isn't to feed your ego. It's to be grateful for your abilities and what already lives inside of you that you were born with. What have you created in your life that you love and are grateful for?

I'm Grateful For:

1. ____________________
2. ____________________
3. ____________________
4. ____________________
5. ____________________
6. ____________________
7. ____________________
8. ____________________
9. ____________________
10. ____________________

Reflections

_/_/_

Signature: ________________

AID STATION #3

One month of daily gratitude. Celebrate that!

Here's what's probably happening:

- The repetition wall is boring.
- Discipline is being tested.
- You're questioning the process.
- Insights are resonating more deeply.

Repetition is habit formation. Do you go to the gym once a week to get the results you want or do you go five to six times? Don't doubt the process, trust it.

For the next ten days, **we're changing the format**.

Instead of listing ten things you're grateful for, list two. Then, write four reasons why for each. If ten is still valuable to you, you can list eight more. Otherwise, we're going narrow and deep for the next ten days. Now go.

Don't forget to text your accountability partner or post. #zeroto54

"Every adversity, every failure, every heartache carries with it the seed of an equal or greater benefit."

Napoleon Hill

Day 30

How do you turn an obstacle into fuel? By saying thank you.

Gratitude can instantly shift your energy if you allow it to resonate. A storm rolled in a few days before I ran my first ultramarathon. Panic turned into inspiration once I expressed gratitude for the mud, rain, and pain because it made the story better. Expressing gratitude for your obstacles enables you to take them on from an empowered state with more energy. They become support rather than resistance. You immediately shift perspective and take back control of your mind.

I acknowledge there are some obstacles that are trivial life problems, like a flat tire. Notwithstanding, what would it look like to respond thoughtfully to life's challenges, even the trivial ones?

I'm Grateful For:

1. ______________________ 6. ______________________

2. ______________________ 7. ______________________

3. ______________________ 8. ______________________

4. ______________________ 9. ______________________

5. ______________________ 10. ______________________

Reflections

__/__/__

Signature: ____________________

Day 31

Daily gratitude can feel boring. How many times have you gone to the same gym to do the same workout?

Going to the gym is a herculean task for someone who doesn't work out regularly. They struggle to develop the habit.

For me, the natural example is the gym and training. For others it could be reading, writing, painting, meditation—anything that requires ongoing commitment to realize maximum benefit. If you don't do it regularly it's hard. Gratitude is no different.

It's consistency of process that produces results. You don't do it because it's always exciting, you do it because it works.

Are there areas of your life where you execute consistently and can leverage that same mentality to maintain your gratitude practice? If not, perhaps this journal can be the first of many.

I'm Grateful For:

1. ______	6. ______
2. ______	7. ______
3. ______	8. ______
4. ______	9. ______
5. ______	10. ______

Reflections

_/_/_

Signature: ________________

Day 32

What do humility, prayer, peace, and presence have in common? They all link to gratitude.

Humility: Acknowledging how we rely on others—the friend who listens, the stranger who helps, or the family who always shows up—evokes gratitude for their support.
Prayer: Slowing down to name our blessings and give thanks for what fills our lives is an expression of gratitude.
Inner peace: Gratitude brings awareness to what we already have, easing our worries.
Presence: Focusing on the present moment creates space to acknowledge the daily blessings we might take for granted.

Which of these areas needs your attention most?

I'm Grateful For:

1. ______________________
2. ______________________
3. ______________________
4. ______________________
5. ______________________
6. ______________________
7. ______________________
8. ______________________
9. ______________________
10. ______________________

Reflections

_/_/_

Signature: ________________

Day 33

Gold is purest when it's melted. Embrace difficulty with gratitude for the opportunity to shine.

Let's lean more into the idea of gratitude for challenges and struggles, the appreciation that hard seasons are opportunities to shine and reveal our true character. It's a universal truth that someone is always fighting a battle you know nothing about. Can you see how yours is an opportunity to put your strength on display? Display it for yourself and no one else. This is *your* journey.

What challenge is currently refining you? How is it creating opportunities to bring out your best and reveal hidden strength?

I'm Grateful For:

1. ____________________
2. ____________________
3. ____________________
4. ____________________
5. ____________________
6. ____________________
7. ____________________
8. ____________________
9. ____________________
10. ____________________

Reflections

__/__/__

Signature: __________________

Day 34

Gratitude, faith, and process. Rinse and repeat.

Gratitude for where you are and what you have. Faith in where you're going and what's coming. Consistent execution of your process to get you there. Remember, gratitude is a tool, and it's not the only one you need in life. I've found that gratitude pairs well with faith and a consistent process.

Do you have faith that your actions will produce results? That God and the universe are helping you? What would your process look like if it were overlaid with faith and gratitude? Would you have more certainty? Feel more energized?

I'm Grateful For:

1. ______	6. ______
2. ______	7. ______
3. ______	8. ______
4. ______	9. ______
5. ______	10. ______

Reflections

_/_/_

Signature: ________________

Day 35

A) Go through a hard season with bitterness.

B) Go through a hard season with gratitude for the opportunity to level up and transform.

You choose.

Difficult seasons are opportunities to level up, and there's gratitude to be found in that. We can't control what happens to us or what cards we're dealt, but we can always choose how to respond.

What hard season are you in right now? Who do you want to be on the other side of this? You get to write the story.

I'm Grateful For:

1. ______________	6. ______________
2. ______________	7. ______________
3. ______________	8. ______________
4. ______________	9. ______________
5. ______________	10. ______________

Reflections

_/_/_

Signature: ____________

Day 36

A grateful mind enhances life's experience. Smile more, embrace more, appreciate more, and ultimately receive more. Like attracts like.

If you show a friend appreciation for all they do and compassion when they go through a hard time, they give more to your relationship and reciprocate. Life works the same way. Appreciate your life, embrace challenges with understanding and compassion, and positivity will be attracted to that.

Today, smile a little more than usual, hold the door open for someone, and look for opportunities to express kind gestures. Notice the subtle energy shifts. When you do, express gratitude for that energy. What kind gestures will you commit to today?

I'm Grateful For:

1. ____________________ 6. ____________________

2. ____________________ 7. ____________________

3. ____________________ 8. ____________________

4. ____________________ 9. ____________________

5. ____________________ 10. ____________________

Reflections

__/__/__

Signature: ____________________

Day 37

There are levels to gratitude where challenges and joys are experienced interconnected rather than stand alone.

Practicing daily gratitude taught me that challenges and struggles lead to immense happiness. The struggle is what makes the achievement meaningful. With that awareness, you can go through difficult situations with gratitude and curiosity for the joy they'll bring. Gratitude becomes possible irrespective of circumstances. In fact, during a difficult time is when it's most important.

Can you reflect on an achievement in your life that would not carry the fulfillment it does had you not struggled and fought for it?

I'm Grateful For:

1. ______________________
2. ______________________
3. ______________________
4. ______________________
5. ______________________
6. ______________________
7. ______________________
8. ______________________
9. ______________________
10. ______________________

Reflections

_/_/_

Signature: ____________________

Day 38

My greatest fear in life is lying on my deathbed wishing I had taken action and realizing it's too late. There's gratitude in something as simple as time. Run your mountain.

I think everyone ought to challenge themselves to run *their* "mountain". By that I mean chase a big dream or goal. One that requires transformation, growth, pain, and struggle and results in one hell of a view from the top. One that you can look back on one day and say, "Fuck yes—*I* did that!"

Get it while you can. Shoot your shot. Embrace failure. Whatever you need to hear, just go for it. If you're still breathing, you still have time. What dream will you decide to pursue today? Express gratitude for the time you have to pursue it.

I'm Grateful For:

1. ______________________ 6. ______________________

2. ______________________ 7. ______________________

3. ______________________ 8. ______________________

4. ______________________ 9. ______________________

5. ______________________ 10. ______________________

Reflections

__/__/__

Signature: ________________

Day 39

Take aim. Move forward with grit, gratitude, and faith, and the path to the summit unfolds faster.

Expressing gratitude for challenges and joys alike requires acceptance. Acceptance for what you can't control allows you to hear your inner voice more clearly and minimizes the mental noise of stress and reluctance. That clarity helps you make better decisions (aim). Once you've established a good and worthwhile aim, have faith that God and His/the universe want you to get there, because they do. Find gratitude for the challenges that come into your life to develop you. Believe in yourself. The higher you aim, the steeper the climb.

What's a worthwhile aim you'll take today? Why is it worthwhile? Does it benefit others as well, or just you?

I'm Grateful For:

1. ______	6. ______
2. ______	7. ______
3. ______	8. ______
4. ______	9. ______
5. ______	10. ______

Reflections

_/_/_

Signature: ________________

AID STATION #4

You're still here, well done. Let's take inventory:

- You've pushed past the initial walls and questions.
- Insights are landing and you might have started realizing that ten gratitudes isn't enough.
- Challenges haven't disappeared, but your relationship to them is changing—at a minimum being questioned.
- The test of discipline occasionally rears its head. Some days are easy while others take more effort.

Here's the truth: if you've made it this far, you have the foundation of a habit, but the cement hasn't fully dried. Is your gratitude homework that stays in the journal, or do you live it throughout your day?

For the next ten-day stretch, continue narrow and deep or go back to listing ten things you're grateful for if that was more helpful. Let your inner voice guide you. Use the theme index if you need to change things up. This next stretch is about agency.

Text your accountability partner or post that you made it to Aid Station #4 with #zeroto54 and keep going. Ten more days.

"The greatest blessings of mankind are within us and within our reach. A wise man is content with his lot, whatever it may be, without wishing for what he has not."

Seneca

Day 40

It's the 12th rep of the 4th set that builds muscle. It's finding gratitude in the depths of struggle that builds mental strength.

Gratitude goes beyond appreciating what you have. It's a tool to reframe a situation. Maybe someone left you, rejected you, a deal fell through, injury, or whatever it may be. Sometimes the universe locks all the doors until you knock on the one it wants you to open. There's gratitude in that. We need failures to make us better because we don't build mental strength when times are good, we build it in the depths of struggle.

Keep faith. Find gratitude. Build grit. What's your current struggle and where is there gratitude waiting to be found?

I'm Grateful For:

1. ______________________ 6. ______________________

2. ______________________ 7. ______________________

3. ______________________ 8. ______________________

4. ______________________ 9. ______________________

5. ______________________ 10. ______________________

Reflections

_/_/_

Signature: ________________

Day 41

If you can't find gratitude, create it. Look for the smallest win or the simplest convenience, then imagine your life without it.

Imagine life without your gym, friends, getting better at your craft, or something as simple as receiving appreciation from others.

There are plenty of times I don't want to run the mountain, but then I think, *What if it wasn't there and I couldn't?* Energy will shift. What's supporting your life that, if it were removed, would make your circumstances difficult?

I'm Grateful For:

1. ______	6. ______
2. ______	7. ______
3. ______	8. ______
4. ______	9. ______
5. ______	10. ______

Reflections

_/_/_

Signature: __________________

Day 42

Yes, the grass is greener where you water it. And the water is gratitude.

Single people want a relationship; coupled people want space. Young people want wisdom and experience; older people want youth. Famous people wish to be anonymous; anonymous people wish to be famous. But how many people are looking for gratitude in what they have?

Do you find yourself in any of these paradoxes? Slow down and reflect that someone wishes they were in your situation. Where is the gratitude in your phase of life? What do you need to water with gratitude?

I'm Grateful For:

1. ______________________
2. ______________________
3. ______________________
4. ______________________
5. ______________________
6. ______________________
7. ______________________
8. ______________________
9. ______________________
10. ______________________

Reflections

_/_/_

Signature: ________________

Day 43

A constant state of gratitude and optimism doesn't eliminate problems; it just lightens the load a lot.

Optimism and gratitude can change how we perceive problems and improve emotional resilience. Instead of seeing problems as insurmountable, they become opportunities for growth, like an unexpected teacher. This fosters an actionable mindset and creates breathing room for creativity and resourcefulness.

The goal isn't to deny reality or our feelings and circumstances. It's to use gratitude as a tool to navigate the negative ones and reorient your mind in a positive direction.

How will you remind yourself to practice gratitude next time the weight on your shoulders feels too heavy? It could be as simple as reading your previous entries.

I'm Grateful For:

1. ______________________________
2. ______________________________
3. ______________________________
4. ______________________________
5. ______________________________
6. ______________________________
7. ______________________________
8. ______________________________
9. ______________________________
10. ______________________________

Reflections

__/__/__

Signature: ________________

Day 44

Gratitude isn't the thankful surface. It's the deep enduring appreciation of blessings and support in your life.

What's the difference between thankful and grateful? They are similar but not the same. Gratitude runs deeper. You might be thankful for a coworker's help but grateful for your family's unwavering love.

You can try what I like to call the "remove-it-from-your-life" test. Think of the things you love in your life. Which ones can you live without and which can you not?

If you can live without it, that's probably thankful. If it's hard to imagine life without it, if it's enduring, that's probably gratitude. Reflect on the differences in your life.

I'm Grateful For:

1. ______________________________
2. ______________________________
3. ______________________________
4. ______________________________
5. ______________________________
6. ______________________________
7. ______________________________
8. ______________________________
9. ______________________________
10. ______________________________

Reflections

_/_/_

Signature: ________________

Day 45

Gratitude is a two-way street.

Expressing gratitude for gifts received not only uplifts you, but the giver as well. Imagine hosting a party and a guest walks in with a gift bag. You accept it and put it on a table with all the others.

Now imagine the same scenario but instead, you take a few moments to acknowledge what the gift is and what it means to you, and express gratitude for the thoughtfulness, time, and effort your guest put into it. You'll feel a greater sense of joy for being seen as will they for being acknowledged. Gratitude multiplies the gift.

How many gifts do we receive and put on a table without acknowledgement? Today, think of three gifts you haven't fully acknowledged. Maybe it's the friend who's always there, your child who wants to spend time with you, or the paid professional who goes above and beyond to give you more than you expect.

I'm Grateful For:

1. ______________________
2. ______________________
3. ______________________
4. ______________________
5. ______________________
6. ______________________
7. ______________________
8. ______________________
9. ______________________
10. ______________________

Reflections

__/__/__

Signature: ________________

Day 46

Gratitude for struggles doesn't mean forcing positivity. It's the appreciation and awareness that you'll emerge stronger and wiser.

Have you ever looked back on a tough time in your life and thought, "I don't want to go through that again, but I love how much I learned and grew from it." Having that awareness in the midst of a tough time—or when you see it coming—can bring a bit of gratitude that also carries hope. There's the potential for a deep appreciation of who's going to come out on the other side. And that's something you can choose to look forward to.

Today, I encourage you to look back on those times and reflect on the version of you that emerged from those difficult seasons. What comes to mind?

I'm Grateful For:

1. ______________________
2. ______________________
3. ______________________
4. ______________________
5. ______________________
6. ______________________
7. ______________________
8. ______________________
9. ______________________
10. ______________________

Reflections

_/_/_

Signature: ____________________

Day 47

Nature's enduring perfection has sunshine and tsunamis. Likewise, our perfection comes from joys and challenges. In seeing that, a grateful mind can form.

Hurricanes, tsunamis, and volcanoes are not pleasurable experiences if you're caught in them, but they're part of nature's balance that has endured forever. Likewise, our joys and challenges are also a balance. Without struggles, we wouldn't evolve. Joys would be bland like food without spice. With that awareness, you can rise above the hardship and see the value in all experiences—they're interconnected.

It's the whole that makes life complete, so why do we only express gratitude for half? Where in your life are you only expressing gratitude for half of the experience? Notice the difficult process that brought the joyful outcome.

I'm Grateful For:

1. ______________ 6. ______________

2. ______________ 7. ______________

3. ______________ 8. ______________

4. ______________ 9. ______________

5. ______________ 10. ______________

Reflections

_/_/_

Signature: ____________________

Day 48

Obstacles are necessary for any successful journey. Approach them with gratitude for the purpose they serve.

Challenges weed out the uncommitted and the quitters. They force us to grow, adapt, build character, develop skills, and discover strengths we didn't know we had. Anything worth doing *successfully* requires struggling well and upward. Gratitude for the process shifts the mindset from frustration to opportunity.

Whatever it is you're fighting for right now, ask yourself, how bad do you want it, and are you prepared to endure transforming into the person able to attain that goal? Which obstacles can you be grateful for and why?

I'm Grateful For:

1. ____________________
2. ____________________
3. ____________________
4. ____________________
5. ____________________
6. ____________________
7. ____________________
8. ____________________
9. ____________________
10. ____________________

Reflections

_/_/_

Signature: __________________

Day 49

Gratitude is freedom. It's taking control of your mental and emotional state from nature's default fearful wiring.

Nature wired us to see fear, by default, for survival. Fast forward to today, we default to what's not working, what we don't have, or what we haven't achieved. Fearful that we may never [insert whatever you want]. Gratitude hijacks this wiring to see what's working for us and empowers a positive outlook and a proactive, rather than reactive, experience.

Yes, some days it's a herculean effort to be grateful, and it feels "better" to sit in fear. But choosing gratitude in those moments is literally when growth happens. It's in that painful moment that your brain is slowly rewiring, like stretching a really tight muscle. Which fearful patterns will you commit to begin breaking today?

I'm Grateful For:

1. ______________________
2. ______________________
3. ______________________
4. ______________________
5. ______________________
6. ______________________
7. ______________________
8. ______________________
9. ______________________
10. ______________________

Reflections

__/__/__

Signature: ________________

AID STATION #5

50 days of daily gratitude and journaling is no small feat! It's not the ten to fifteen minutes a day, it's the consistent execution.

By now you've passed the survival stage and are entering deeper transformation toward a grateful mind. You've had mornings of exuberance, and mornings of checking a box, days of feeling plateaued, and days of hoping for more aha moments. But your baseline has shifted—you're noticing more gratitude than when you started.

And those plateaus? The days where something feels like it's still missing? Those are signals pointing you toward what only you can uncover. Gratitude strips away the noise and reveals the misalignment in your life, but it's up to you to keep looking.

Where are you today, at the halfway mark, in relation to the person who started Day 1? Reflect on the journey for a moment and honor how far you've come.

Moving forward, it's back to ten gratitudes per day. Narrow and deep was an exercise to experience how far gratitude can go.

We're going to keep discovering your values, identifying the misalignment in your life, and stretching your gratitude.

Remember, ten days at a time. Text your accountability partner or post on social and keep marching.

"If an egg is broken by outside force, Life ends. If broken by inside force, Life begins. Great things always begin from inside."

Jim Kwik

Day 50

We are all given 24 hours in a day, except the last one. Reflect on each day with gratitude for the blessing of time.

We never know which day we'll get shorted. Morning or evening reflections are mental preparations for the day to come. It's no different than meal prepping, getting your clothes ready, or tidying your house. Prep your mind with gratitude because it empowers you to play all out and show up as your best self.

Gratitude isn't just for waking up, but for going to bed as well. What if today was your last day? What would you want it to look like? Can you design it right now? List three experiences that are non-negotiable today.

I'm Grateful For:

1. ____________________ 6. ____________________

2. ____________________ 7. ____________________

3. ____________________ 8. ____________________

4. ____________________ 9. ____________________

5. ____________________ 10. ____________________

Reflections

_/_/_

Signature: ________________

Day 51

Gratitude is a response, not a reaction.

A reaction is quick and emotional, without much control, triggered by an external stimulus.

A response is thoughtful, intentional, and measured. Gratitude doesn't come naturally. It's a deliberate practice that needs to be cultivated over time. As you go through your day, notice whether you are reacting or responding. Thoughtfulness requires slowing down and sitting in the space between stimulus and response.

What are some things or people that trigger you? Next time you're triggered, slow down and give yourself grace. It's okay to be upset. And then realize you can express gratitude for the trigger because it's showing you where you need to grow.

I'm Grateful For:

1. ______________	6. ______________
2. ______________	7. ______________
3. ______________	8. ______________
4. ______________	9. ______________
5. ______________	10. ______________

Reflections

_/_/_

Signature: ________________

Day 52

Gratitude fosters creation. We create from abundance, not scarcity or lack.

Gratitude shifts your mind from what's not working to what is, from what you don't have to what you do, and helps you find value in difficult situations. Those are catalysts to building anything meaningful. It's difficult to create from a negative, closed, or discouraged state. Positivity encourages progress, which leads to creation.

What's a situation you're going through that could benefit from reframing and a different perspective? Can you imagine yourself overcoming the challenge and creating something meaningful? Do challenges exist to inhibit creation or guide it?

I'm Grateful For:

1. ______________________
2. ______________________
3. ______________________
4. ______________________
5. ______________________
6. ______________________
7. ______________________
8. ______________________
9. ______________________
10. ______________________

Reflections

_/_/_

Signature: __________________

Day 53

Ask yourself, who or what supported me yesterday? That's your morning gratitude.

Sometimes it's just asking the right questions that makes the difference.

I'm Grateful For:

1. ______________________
2. ______________________
3. ______________________
4. ______________________
5. ______________________
6. ______________________
7. ______________________
8. ______________________
9. ______________________
10. ______________________

Reflections

__/__/__

Signature: ____________

Day 54

In 1913, J.D. Rockefeller had $900 million. Today, you live better than he did. Think of the gratitude in that.

I'm not one to compare, but perspective is important. There's so much gratitude to be had in our lives that we take for granted. A near billionaire in 1913 didn't have a refrigerator, washing machine, antibiotics, ibuprofen, air conditioning, cell phones, or other conveniences we forget to appreciate. Let that sink in.

How does this perspective make you feel? Does it encourage you to view your life differently? Which modern conveniences help you to appreciate being alive at this time in history?

I'm Grateful For:

1. ______________________________
2. ______________________________
3. ______________________________
4. ______________________________
5. ______________________________
6. ______________________________
7. ______________________________
8. ______________________________
9. ______________________________
10. ______________________________

Reflections

_/_/_

Signature: ________________

Day 55

The hedonic treadmill: people quickly adapt to wins and return to their baseline of happiness. Unless they practice gratitude.

Coined by Philip Brickman and Donald Campbell in 1971, the hedonic treadmill theory suggests that people are generally quick to get over the surge of happiness that comes from a big win or event in their lives. We return to our baseline of happiness as the wins become our new normal.

Think of the joy we experience from getting a raise or buying something new, and how that fades over time. A gratitude practice counteracts that, can remind us of the joy we first experienced with the win or purchase, and what life was like before it.

Name three things that excited you to the moon at first, but your initial enthusiasm has since faded. Can you find the capacity to express gratitude for them again?

I'm Grateful For:

1. ______________________ 6. ______________________

2. ______________________ 7. ______________________

3. ______________________ 8. ______________________

4. ______________________ 9. ______________________

5. ______________________ 10. ______________________

Reflections

_/_/_

Signature: ____________________

Day 56

A. List your gratitude when it feels good.
B. List your gratitude every day regardless.
What you do, and when you do it, matters.

Anyone can be grateful when life feels good. But are you a plastic bag in the wind, or are you in the driver's seat of your mind and emotions? What word, phrase, or action can you use to anchor yourself in gratitude regardless of circumstances?

I'm Grateful For:

1. ______	6. ______
2. ______	7. ______
3. ______	8. ______
4. ______	9. ______
5. ______	10. ______

Reflections

_/_/_

Signature: ________________

Day 57

Genuine gratitude sees the world interconnected. Challenges exist for your benefit. Once you see that, you progress much faster.

I believe the deepest joys in life would lack their depth had they been handed to us. Putting in the work is what gives victory substance by providing contrast.

Gratitude for challenges is the awareness that they exist to transform you into the person who can achieve the goals you set for yourself. Gratitude for the interplay of struggle and joy is how you see the world interconnected.

How are your struggles developing you into a stronger and wiser person? How do you imagine yourself when you come out the other side? Describe that person, then notice which challenges in your life are shaping that person?

I'm Grateful For:

1. ______________________
2. ______________________
3. ______________________
4. ______________________
5. ______________________
6. ______________________
7. ______________________
8. ______________________
9. ______________________
10. ______________________

Reflections

_/_/_

Signature: __________________

Day 58

What you put into life is what you get out. Put more gratitude in, get more reasons for gratitude out.

Put more time in the gym, get a better mind and body. Put more time into your relationships, get more fulfillment. Put more work toward your goals, find more success. Express more gratitude for the joys and challenges in life, progress further, faster, and happier as the gratitude compounds through daily practice.

Yes, there are times we don't get the outcome we wanted. But that doesn't mean there isn't something else to be gained. How much gratitude can you put into your day today? Find five opportunities throughout the day to say, "I'm grateful for [insert support]."

I'm Grateful For:

1. ______________________ 6. ______________________

2. ______________________ 7. ______________________

3. ______________________ 8. ______________________

4. ______________________ 9. ______________________

5. ______________________ 10. ______________________

Reflections

__/__/__

Signature: ________________

Day 59

When you get bad news, keep looking for gratitude until you find it. It's there, even if it's unpleasant.

Once the bad news is processed, take a step back and look at the situation in its entirety. Look for reasons why it might be better this way and remind yourself that the story isn't over. Somewhere in there you'll find gratitude, even if just a little. And that will help you progress faster and further. I promise. *(Remember, there's no gratitude for tragedies or loss of life. Grace before gratitude.)*

Is there an area of your life that's struggling or has fallen apart? Can you slow down to dig for the gratitude in it? Find three.

I'm Grateful For:

1. ______________________ 6. ______________________

2. ______________________ 7. ______________________

3. ______________________ 8. ______________________

4. ______________________ 9. ______________________

5. ______________________ 10. ______________________

Reflections

_/_/_

Signature: ________________

AID STATION #6

You're in the thick of it. If you're experiencing a lack of motivation I want you to remember, discipline does what motivation can't. No one who runs an ultramarathon feels motivated between miles 50 and 80. They move forward because they made a commitment to themselves. The reward can only be reaped at the finish line.

Here's where you might be:

- It feels strange to skip. The habit is locking in.
- You're noticing that gratitude isn't a feeling, it's a state.
- Your core values are showing up in the repetition.
- Part of you might be wondering: "Why forty more days?"

Here's why: we want it to become second nature. The next forty are about deepening your understanding of gratitude, revealing misalignment through emptiness, and preventing drift back into your old lens.

Take a moment to look back at Days 1 through 60. What keeps showing up on your list? Where does emptiness linger? Pull on those threads.

In ten more days, you'll enter Phase 3: Mastery. Until then, don't negotiate with yourself. Keep showing up.

Text your accountability partner or post on social and get to your gratitude. #zeroto54

"Do not spoil what you have by desiring what you have not; remember that what you now have was once among the things you only hoped for."

Epicurus

Day 60

"Our lives are given to us. Therefore, our default state should be gratitude."

Unknown

Take a minute to let this sink in.

Gratitude is for the things given to us. Things we did nothing to earn but received anyway such as help from friends, grace and compassion from others, challenges that show up to teach us strength and patience, and of course, our lives.

What are the blessings and love that show up in your life as pure gifts to you from others? Who has shown up for you selflessly?

I'm Grateful For:

1. ______________________
2. ______________________
3. ______________________
4. ______________________
5. ______________________
6. ______________________
7. ______________________
8. ______________________
9. ______________________
10. ______________________

Reflections

_/_/_

Signature: ____________________

Day 61

Gratitude is like compound interest. Small daily deposits become a gift that keeps on giving.

Do you have days where you feel like progress isn't being made? That's okay, and that's normal. Keep making deposits. Think of gratitude like saving a small amount of money every day. At the end of the year, you'll have a nice cushion. A grateful mind doesn't develop overnight. Keep chipping away at it, especially when it's hard.

What little deposits will you make today? As you go about your day, look for the smallest experiences to be grateful for.

I'm Grateful For:

1. ______________________ 6. ______________________

2. ______________________ 7. ______________________

3. ______________________ 8. ______________________

4. ______________________ 9. ______________________

5. ______________________ 10. ______________________

Reflections

_/_/_

____

____

____

____

____

____

____

____

____

____

____

____

____

____

____

____

____

____

____

Signature: ____________________

Day 62

Evolution has no destination. Challenges and joys are stepping stones to becoming your best until you die. Gratitude is how you enjoy the journey.

The cycle of joys and struggles empowers forward progress to the highest version of yourself. Once you realize that and find gratitude in the process (especially during hardship), you find peace.

Think of a challenge in your life like an escape room. You need to find the clues to get yourself out. When you solve it, you become wiser, stronger, and able to help others.

Where will you look for clues today? Where are the challenges (hints) guiding you? Is it to become stronger or to move in a different direction?

I'm Grateful For:

1. ______________________
2. ______________________
3. ______________________
4. ______________________
5. ______________________
6. ______________________
7. ______________________
8. ______________________
9. ______________________
10. ______________________

Reflections

__/__/__

Signature: ____________________

Day 63

Grit and gratitude are a powerful combination. Grit keeps you going; gratitude keeps you present.

What would happen if you had resiliency and a mind grounded in the abundance of the present moment? First, you'd discover how unstoppable you are. Second, you'd probably start to expand your mind as to what's achievable. Third, you'd probably start aiming a lot higher. Fourth is up to you. But make no mistake, you'll need plenty of grit and gratitude to achieve bigger goals.

On day 63, it's clear that you have grit and gratitude. How can you expand it? Where are you currently aiming, and is it high enough? Are you maximizing your potential or leaving some on the table? What are three areas in your life where you can apply 10 percent more?

I'm Grateful For:

1. ____________________
2. ____________________
3. ____________________
4. ____________________
5. ____________________
6. ____________________
7. ____________________
8. ____________________
9. ____________________
10. ____________________

Reflections

_/_/_

Signature: __________________

Day 64

Today is the greatest time in history to be alive, but happiness has trended down in the West. Is gratitude missing?

According to Gallup polls and the World Happiness Report (2024), happiness has trended down in the West despite a high quality of life. Social media and society broadly encourage the chase for more which, by definition, implies that we are lacking. It's not in corporate interest to focus on the abundance you already have. But the truth is we're not lacking.

As gratitude becomes more ingrained in your life, you can begin to notice the blessings in the lives of others as well. Focus on the gratitude around you. If you can participate in the joy of gratitude in the lives of others, that's a sign of deep understanding. Today, look for three opportunities to notice gratitude (gifts received) in someone else's life.

I'm Grateful For:

1. ______________________
2. ______________________
3. ______________________
4. ______________________
5. ______________________
6. ______________________
7. ______________________
8. ______________________
9. ______________________
10. ______________________

Reflections

_/_/_

Signature: ________________

Day 65

Next time your mindset is off, list ten gratitudes. It will uplift you, even if just a little. I promise.

Are there days when you're not feeling particularly grateful, or wondering when your path will finally open for you? Sometimes it's not enough to just list your gratitude in the morning. Anytime you find yourself drifting into a negative space—pause. List ten things you're grateful for, or more, because gratitude and negativity cannot coexist.

Will you discipline your mind and stick with your gratitude practice, or let events outside of you control you? What's a current challenge in your life that causes you to struggle? Next time it comes up, commit to listing ten gratitudes and watch what happens to your state.

I'm Grateful For:

1. ______________________
2. ______________________
3. ______________________
4. ______________________
5. ______________________
6. ______________________
7. ______________________
8. ______________________
9. ______________________
10. ______________________

Reflections

__/__/__

Signature: __________________

Day 66

Gratitude leads to truth about reality. It's like wiping the lens on your camera so you can see what is.

Approach life with gratitude so you can see it more clearly, as it truly is, instead of our natural tendencies to see what isn't. In a relationship, for example, you might be focused on what your partner isn't doing. But did you express gratitude for the things they are doing that you might have gotten used to? Or can you see how your struggles are strengthening you to achieve your goals? There's a grounding effect in gratitude.

How long will you continue to focus on what's missing rather than what's already there? In your reflection today, list five things you believe are missing in your life. Then list five things you have—counter to what's missing—that you've overlooked or gotten used to.

I'm Grateful For:

1. ____________	6. ____________
2. ____________	7. ____________
3. ____________	8. ____________
4. ____________	9. ____________
5. ____________	10. ____________

Reflections

__/__/__

Signature: ________________

Day 67

Transformation is painful. Choose your change wisely, and take your gratitude prescription: written, once daily upon waking.

We all go through change (at least I hope you do), and it's often painful because you're challenging your existing beliefs, habits, or perceptions. Finding gratitude during transformation gives you power. How? By giving it a sense of purpose. Gratitude for what's being built, the wisdom being gained, and the support (whatever shape it takes) in your life that's helping you transform. Like taking ibuprofen for a bad headache—feel the ache, embrace gratitude, keep going.

Could gratitude be the key to unlocking a more authentic version of yourself? Whatever challenges you experience today, let your first question be, "How can I get better from this? Where is the gratitude?"

I'm Grateful For:

1. ______________________________ 6. ______________________________

2. ______________________________ 7. ______________________________

3. ______________________________ 8. ______________________________

4. ______________________________ 9. ______________________________

5. ______________________________ 10. ______________________________

Reflections

_/_/_

____

____

____

____

____

____

____

____

____

____

____

____

____

____

____

____

____

____

____

Signature: ____________________

Day 68

Gratitude doesn't eliminate hard days; it armors your mind to handle them.

It's hard to focus on your blessings when you're not where you want to be or have experienced a significant change or setback in your life. Practicing gratitude in these moments is incredibly hard, but that's when it matters most. One by one, get to ten. The longer it takes, the longer you've spent focusing on your blessings. If you're feeling lost, gratitude can help you find your way by reconnecting you to what matters most.

What support exists within your current struggle that you haven't acknowledged yet? A lesson, a strength being built, a door you wouldn't have found if you didn't have to keep knocking?

I'm Grateful For:

1. ______________________
2. ______________________
3. ______________________
4. ______________________
5. ______________________
6. ______________________
7. ______________________
8. ______________________
9. ______________________
10. ______________________

Reflections

_/_/_

Signature: ________________

Day 69

God doesn't give you what you want; He gives you what you need to get what you want. And it usually comes as a struggle. With that awareness, we find gratitude in it.

If you're aiming up toward something better—a relationship, a level of income, or a personal record—and were the person who knew how to attain it, you'd already have it. But you don't, so you need to transform.

Well, that's painful. But if you're aware of the process happening, can *hold* that awareness at the forefront, and express gratitude for it, it becomes much easier to endure.

What's an anchor you can develop that grounds you in awareness of the process? How will you commit to reminding yourself that your struggles are making you better?

I'm Grateful For:

1. __________	6. __________
2. __________	7. __________
3. __________	8. __________
4. __________	9. __________
5. __________	10. __________

Reflections

_/_/_

Signature: ____________________

PHASE THREE

MASTERY

THE GRATEFUL MIND

(31 DAYS)

Welcome to Phase 3 (and Aid Station #7): Mastery.

Seventy days. The habit is yours, and here's what you're *likely* experiencing:

- Gratitude feels more like a lens to see the world through.
- You notice it randomly throughout your day.
- Negativity fades faster and you recover quicker than you used to.
- Your relationships carry more empathy and presence.
- Challenges don't derail you the way they used to.

Be mindful that the shifts from a daily gratitude practice are subtle. It's not a state of constant exuberance. You'll notice it if you slow down to reflect on your old patterns compared to where you are now. It's the frog in water that doesn't realize it ever so slowly came to a boil.

The next thirty days are about understanding gratitude at a deeper level and ingraining it in a way that feels off if you don't practice. The goal is to solidify the difference in your life before and after gratitude. Do your accountability check-in and move on.

"When you activate gratitude and practice it in your life, you'll notice that there is more and more to be grateful for every single moment. You will begin to live in this state of gratitude—this is how you continuously cultivate a beautiful state."

Tony Robbins

Day 70

Sincere gratitude is invincible.

Sincere gratitude, cultivated at your core, is invincible. Meaning it becomes unshakable no matter your circumstances. Your mind learns to look for gratitude even in the midst of challenges, and hopefully, even for the challenge itself. It gives you resiliency in adversity, improves emotional well-being, strengthens relationships, and improves inner peace when cultivated daily. Writing, I believe, is the best way because it forces you to articulate your thoughts and slow down—both of which enhance emotional processing.

Today, if you're not already, indicate "why" next to each gratitude and notice the difference. Use the reflection page if you need more space.

I'm Grateful For:

1. ______________________ 6. ______________________

2. ______________________ 7. ______________________

3. ______________________ 8. ______________________

4. ______________________ 9. ______________________

5. ______________________ 10. ______________________

Reflections

_/_/_

Signature: ________________

Day 71

Gratitude can't coexist with fear and anger. You choose.

If you're focused on the blessings you have today, your mind can't simultaneously be anxious about something in the future (fear) or ruminating about the past (regret). Practicing gratitude creates peace (even if just for the time you're focused on it), and the goal is to expand that peace as much as possible. Fear and love compete for the same mental space.

What's one single gratitude you can use to find a moment of peace whenever you need it? Something that resonates deeply, you're fortunate to have, and is fundamentally important to who you are.

I'm Grateful For:

1. ______________________ 6. ______________________

2. ______________________ 7. ______________________

3. ______________________ 8. ______________________

4. ______________________ 9. ______________________

5. ______________________ 10. ______________________

Reflections

_/_/_

Signature: ________________

Day 72

How do you feel when someone gives you genuine gratitude and appreciation? Be that someone.

While you benefit the most from practicing gratitude, it's not just for you. It benefits everyone around you because it's a two-way street. Expressing gratitude benefits both you and the giver. Today, be the reason for gratitude in someone's life. Maybe buy the person in line behind you a coffee or give a stranger a compliment; look for the smallest way to spread gratitude and positivity. You will benefit the most because you were the reason for a human connection and a joyful memory.

Commit to three ways you will be the gratitude in someone else's life today. What would happen if you did that every day?

I'm Grateful For:

1. ______________________ 6. ______________________

2. ______________________ 7. ______________________

3. ______________________ 8. ______________________

4. ______________________ 9. ______________________

5. ______________________ 10. ______________________

Reflections

_/_/_

Signature: __________________

Day 73

No matter what happens, and no matter how hard, find gratitude.

Period. Gratitude doesn't eliminate challenges or circumstances. It's just a tool to reframe your mind, uplift your energy, and get you through a difficult situation faster. Process however you need to, but don't let the negativity breathe too much because that's where most people falter. They forget this is just a moment in time. The hardship is temporary, but the gifts and blessings in your life have always been there.

How active are you in noticing when negativity is breathing too much? Are you processing with awareness or letting it run its course unchecked? A grateful mind processes, then chooses when to pivot.

Today, think of a hardship you're facing and ask yourself: has it been given its due? If so, look for gratitude for what it's taught you. Say thank you and move on.

I'm Grateful For:

1. ____________________ 6. ____________________

2. ____________________ 7. ____________________

3. ____________________ 8. ____________________

4. ____________________ 9. ____________________

5. ____________________ 10. ____________________

Reflections

_/_/_

Signature: ________________

Day 74

You own your mind free and clear. Choose your thoughts. Choose to see opportunity, not failure. A bullet dodged, not a door closed. Choose gratitude.

We can make things mean whatever we want them to. Gratitude is truth serum anchored in verifiable facts. "This person rejected me but I'm grateful I wasn't sucked into the wrong relationship." "I didn't win the deal but I'm grateful for what I learned, and my skills are that much better for it." "I lost a client, but I'm grateful for the time I got back."

What are three areas of your life that might need to be assigned a new meaning? How will that change your relationship to them?

I'm Grateful For:

1. ______________________
2. ______________________
3. ______________________
4. ______________________
5. ______________________
6. ______________________
7. ______________________
8. ______________________
9. ______________________
10. ______________________

Reflections

_/_/_

Signature: ________________

Day 75

Practicing gratitude during the good times bears fruit during the hard times.

Practicing daily gratitude when things are going well bulletproofs your mind. You don't realize how resilient it's made you until shit hits the fan. When you inevitably become the recipient of bad news or hardship, your mind is trained to notice what's still working and what's still good in your life. It knows how to flex.

How will you build up your mental reserves and armor your mind today? I challenge you to find as many reasons for gratitude as you can throughout your day, starting with your daily ten. At the end of the day, reflect on your count.

I'm Grateful For:

1. ______________________
2. ______________________
3. ______________________
4. ______________________
5. ______________________
6. ______________________
7. ______________________
8. ______________________
9. ______________________
10. ______________________

Reflections

_/_/_

Signature: ____________________

Day 76

The opposite of gratitude isn't ingratitude, it's ignorance.

This may come off a bit harsh but bear with me. Gratitude is the deep enduring appreciation of support in your life. Support which, were it removed, would make life difficult. Therefore, failing to express gratitude for the blessings and support in your life, no matter how small, is a demonstration of ignorance—a lack of awareness. Even if it feels empty at times, stay aware of your blessings and support.

Does this contrast encourage you to approach gratitude differently? How so?

I'm Grateful For:

1. ______________________
2. ______________________
3. ______________________
4. ______________________
5. ______________________
6. ______________________
7. ______________________
8. ______________________
9. ______________________
10. ______________________

Reflections

_/_/_

Signature: __________________

Day 77

God's noes are like bowling bumpers. They keep you on the path and out of the gutter. Find gratitude in "no."

God and His universe answer all prayers. Just because it's not the answer or timing you want doesn't mean it's not the right answer.

Can you trust that today's "no" is tomorrow's blessing? Think of a recent "no" and think of the possibilities that can emerge as a result. Or think of a time in the past where a "no" led you to a better "yes." In that, we find gratitude.

I'm Grateful For:

1. ______________________
2. ______________________
3. ______________________
4. ______________________
5. ______________________
6. ______________________
7. ______________________
8. ______________________
9. ______________________
10. ______________________

Reflections

_/_/_

Signature: ____________________

Day 78

Gratitude reveals your true values.

When you pay attention to what you're grateful for, you uncover your deepest priorities. There's a reason your mind chose that gratitude. It's a mirror to your soul.

What would you grieve if it were lost? What patterns have you noticed in your gratitude that reflect your values? What recurring themes do you see when you reflect on the last 78 days?

I'm Grateful For:

1. ____________________
2. ____________________
3. ____________________
4. ____________________
5. ____________________
6. ____________________
7. ____________________
8. ____________________
9. ____________________
10. ____________________

Reflections

__/__/__

Signature: ________________

Day 79

Gratitude won't change your circumstances, but it will change your relationship to them.

A subtle shift in perception can alter your entire experience. If we can flip the script to see challenges and struggles as support to develop or guide us, like a parent practicing tough love, we begin to experience difficult situations in a different light. One that encourages positive forward motion.

Remember, this doesn't apply to tragedies. But even in traumatic experiences, there is still gratitude in your life to be found *when you're ready* to look for it. As long as you're alive, the story isn't over.

Where in your life are you challenged? How can you change your relationship to that challenge? Will you control your perspective or be controlled by the challenge?

I'm Grateful For:

1. ______________________
2. ______________________
3. ______________________
4. ______________________
5. ______________________
6. ______________________
7. ______________________
8. ______________________
9. ______________________
10. ______________________

Reflections

_/_/_

Signature: ________________

AID STATION #8

Eighty days of habit building is incredible! That's rarefied air. Here's where you might be:

- Gratitude is your go-to lens when you need perspective.
- You reframe more easily.
- You need less external validation. What you have feels like enough.
- You might be spreading it by noticing others' joys and expressing appreciation more freely.
- The end of this journey is in sight, and part of you is already celebrating.

Here's some food for thought: is the goal to finish these 100 days, or is it to make gratitude a regular daily practice?

If you're feeling mechanical, go deeper and say why. If you're facing hard times, remember grace comes before gratitude. Remind yourself, and be proud, of how far you've come.

Text your accountability partner or post your status #zeroto54. Keep going, the end is in sight.

"Be grateful in spite of your suffering. There's some real utility in gratitude. Gratitude is the process of consciously and courageously attempting thankfulness in the face of the catastrophe of life."

Jordan Peterson

Day 80

Gratitude is acceptance. And that's always the first step in any upward journey.

You can't move forward effectively if you're in denial about where you are. With acceptance, you free up energy that was being used to deny reality. Denial consumes energy, clouds your judgment, and inhibits your ability to execute correctly. But when you tell the truth, especially to yourself, you clear a path forward.

Is there an area of your life that might need some acceptance in order for you to begin to change? Write it out and express gratitude for the awareness.

I'm Grateful For:

1. ______________________________
2. ______________________________
3. ______________________________
4. ______________________________
5. ______________________________
6. ______________________________
7. ______________________________
8. ______________________________
9. ______________________________
10. ______________________________

Reflections

_/_/_

Signature: ________________

Day 81

Water won't boil if you keep turning off the flame. Practice gratitude daily.

You don't get stronger by going to the gym once in a while. Likewise, you don't develop the skill of reframing with gratitude by practicing occasionally. Discipline is the price of transformation. The benefits of a grateful mind can't be realized without consistent daily practice. One of those benefits is that the discipline you've built here is leverage—it can compound in other areas of your life.

What other repeatable daily action will you commit to starting today? What's a habit you've been trying to develop that you can commit to, the way you have with gratitude?

I'm Grateful For:

1. ______________________	6. ______________________
2. ______________________	7. ______________________
3. ______________________	8. ______________________
4. ______________________	9. ______________________
5. ______________________	10. ______________________

Reflections

_/_/_

Signature: __________________

Day 82

Reflect with gratitude on the people who have sacrificed time, energy, and resources to support you. Reflect, and never quit.

By never quitting until you reach your goals, you let them know their time, energy, and resources were not wasted. There are certainly times when it makes sense to call something over; you gave it your all and left no stone unturned. But as long as there's opportunity and a burning desire, keep going. The best "thank you" is crossing the finish line.

Gratitude can remind you of the resources and people rooting for your success. In your reflection, list three people rooting for you, then write how they inspire you.

I'm Grateful For:

1. ______________________
2. ______________________
3. ______________________
4. ______________________
5. ______________________
6. ______________________
7. ______________________
8. ______________________
9. ______________________
10. ______________________

Reflections

__/__/__

Signature: ________________

Day 83

Like roots to a tree, gratitude grounds and nourishes you while you grow.

Our foundation determines whether we stand strong in the face of adversity or topple over when life tests our resilience. Gratitude is the root system anchoring you to your proven capabilities and the abundance in your life.

Who or what are the roots you can reconnect to during turbulence? Is it your family and friends? Faith? Past achievements? All of the above? On the Reflection page, list three anchors you can reconnect to during your next challenge.

I'm Grateful For:

1. ______________________	6. ______________________
2. ______________________	7. ______________________
3. ______________________	8. ______________________
4. ______________________	9. ______________________
5. ______________________	10. ______________________

Reflections

_/_/_

Signature: ____________________

Day 84

Practice daily gratitude to notice blessings that have been there all along.

We're all blessed; we just need to notice it.

Have you noticed repetition in your gratitude? What have you realized you value most? If you could only be grateful for five things for the rest of your life, what would they be?

Once you've reflected on the five things, ask yourself: How much time am I investing in these areas?

I'm Grateful For:

1. ______________________
2. ______________________
3. ______________________
4. ______________________
5. ______________________
6. ______________________
7. ______________________
8. ______________________
9. ______________________
10. ______________________

Reflections

_/_/_

Signature: __________________

Day 85

Gratitude is humility that grounds you in the present. It allows you to see what in life is happening for you, pleasant or not.

Gratitude is humility to subordinate your ego and slow you down to appreciate what's happening for you. To see that challenges and joys are working for you doesn't make life easier—it makes *you* better.

After 85 days of gratitude, have you realized how much you've been given and how supported you are? Which challenges have become opportunities?

I'm Grateful For:

1. ______________________
2. ______________________
3. ______________________
4. ______________________
5. ______________________
6. ______________________
7. ______________________
8. ______________________
9. ______________________
10. ______________________

Reflections

__/__/__

Signature: ____________________

Day 86

Sometimes you might not be in the mood to practice gratitude. Opt for grit, it will lead you back to practicing your gratitude.

We're all human. There are always days we don't feel like showing up. It's how you take that next step that matters. Doing what needs to get done irrespective of your feelings is a sign of mastery. It shows that you're in control of your mind and emotions, not the other way around. Grit and gratitude are a powerful combination.

Do you feel proud of yourself for getting to 86 days? Describe the days you didn't want to show up but did.

I'm Grateful For:

1. ______________________ 6. ______________________

2. ______________________ 7. ______________________

3. ______________________ 8. ______________________

4. ______________________ 9. ______________________

5. ______________________ 10. ______________________

Reflections

_/_/_

Signature: __________________

Day 87

Gratitude transforms suffering into meaning.

Suffering is fertile ground for transformation. If you can find gratitude in the midst of it, you'll slow down enough to find purpose. Because despite the challenges you're facing, you are in receipt of daily gifts, including the challenge itself. That means you're in the arena, and the powers that be believe you are ready for this.

Most people wait until hardship passes to extract meaning from it. They look back and say, "I'm grateful for what that taught me." But a grateful mind doesn't wait. It asks, while still in the fire, "Where is this guiding me? What is it making of me? What can I thank this struggle for, even now?"

Whatever you might be going through, pause. Are you fighting this challenge or flowing with it? What is it trying to teach you, and can you say thank you for that? Remember, grace before gratitude.

I'm Grateful For:

1. ____________________
2. ____________________
3. ____________________
4. ____________________
5. ____________________
6. ____________________
7. ____________________
8. ____________________
9. ____________________
10. ____________________

Reflections

__/__/__

Signature: ____________________

Day 88

Deeply felt gratitude is connective tissue to the world.

Through consistent daily practice, you'll start to notice gratitude in the lives of others. You see the gifts and blessings they receive, or even how their challenges are helping them grow. A grateful mind allows you to share in the joy of that observed gratitude. You see how others are blessed and can participate in their happiness because you now know what it feels like. Once you experience that, you find joy and happiness all around you and realize it's accessible at any time.

Can you notice gratitude in the lives of others, and can you start to feel their joy? Today, look for someone experiencing gratitude. Put yourself in their shoes to appreciate and acknowledge their experience.

I'm Grateful For:

1. ______________________
2. ______________________
3. ______________________
4. ______________________
5. ______________________
6. ______________________
7. ______________________
8. ______________________
9. ______________________
10. ______________________

Reflections

_/_/_

Signature: ________________

Day 89

Pressure doesn't create character, it reveals it. There's gratitude for the opportunities to put it on display.

Pressures of life don't exist to make you miserable; they exist to transform you and provide opportunities to shine. How does a team know it's the best unless it's challenged? A grateful mind empowers you to perform—to prove to yourself what you're capable of.

Is there an area of your life where you're tired? Anyone can show up when it's easy. It's finding the strength to endure when you want to quit that counts. What would it take for you to show up like it's Day 1? Maybe you need to remember who's counting on you, starting with you.

I'm Grateful For:

1. ______________________________
2. ______________________________
3. ______________________________
4. ______________________________
5. ______________________________
6. ______________________________
7. ______________________________
8. ______________________________
9. ______________________________
10. ______________________________

Reflections

__/__/__

Signature: ________________

AID STATION #9

Ninety days. Ten to go. Refuel for the final stretch.

Here's where you might be:

- Gratitude isn't something you do anymore—it's how you think.
- Reframing comes quicker. You catch yourself defaulting to it more easily.
- Presence is high. Anxiety is quieter than it's been in a long time. Not gone, but noticeably lower.
- You're already thinking about what happens after Day 100.

These last ten days aren't about new insights; they're about locking in what you've discovered. It's the beginning of carrying your practice forward without the guidance. The journal was scaffolding. The habit you've built is yours.

You've revealed your values. You've earned your peace. You've gone on one hell of a journey. Now finish what you started. Text your accountability partner or post #zeroto54.

"The struggle ends when gratitude begins."
Neale Donald Walsch

Day 90

Gratitude isn't just being happy and content. It's a steady, uplifting mentality that gets you to your goals faster.

The biggest obstacle to reaching your goals is the inches between your ears. Mastering your mind leads to effective and consistent execution. That's why grit and gratitude are needed together. The greatest progress is made with grounded resilience. Grounding in who you are, what you're capable of, and awareness of the ever-present support—big and small—in your life.

What challenges has gratitude helped you overcome these last 90 days? When difficulty hits, do you feel like you have ground to stand on? Can you notice a subtle calm in your life?

I'm Grateful For:

1. ____________________
2. ____________________
3. ____________________
4. ____________________
5. ____________________
6. ____________________
7. ____________________
8. ____________________
9. ____________________
10. ____________________

Reflections

_/_/_

Signature: __________________

Day 91

Challenges aren't punishments; they're necessities. A grateful mind helps you embrace them.

If you've developed a grateful mind, your capacity has expanded. Maybe you were moving one step at a time, but now you can move two. More transformation can happen for you if you seek it. Challenges that would've flattened you a year ago now feel manageable. Not because they're smaller, but because you have better tools. You have proof. You have 91 days of gratitude, including the days you didn't feel like showing up.

Where do you see this transformation most in your life? What challenges have you been avoiding because they felt too big? Move toward those challenges today. What's the first step?

I'm Grateful For:

1. ____________________ 6. ____________________

2. ____________________ 7. ____________________

3. ____________________ 8. ____________________

4. ____________________ 9. ____________________

5. ____________________ 10. ____________________

Reflections

__/__/__

Signature: ____________________

Day 92

Gratitude isn't about being happy. It's about acceptance and reality. *That's* what leads to happiness.

Building on Day 90, acceptance is the first step in any transformation, so accept all of it. The good, the bad, the things you don't yet understand, and the distance between where you are and where you want to be. Choose to see the blessings that exist today. That's how you choose happiness—by focusing on the right thoughts. From there we build, grow, and embrace the joys and challenges that move us forward.

Are there any uncomfortable truths you haven't accepted? What would happen if you took responsibility and did? Is there gratitude in those truths?

I'm Grateful For:

1. ______________________
2. ______________________
3. ______________________
4. ______________________
5. ______________________
6. ______________________
7. ______________________
8. ______________________
9. ______________________
10. ______________________

Reflections

_/_/_

Signature: ________________

Day 93

Gratitude is humility when you're flying too high and uplifting when you're too low. It centers you.

It's not healthy to sit in overconfidence or a low mood for too long. They feed the ego in different ways—whether that's yay me or woe is me. Take time to celebrate wins or process losses but then ground yourself in gratitude. It reminds you that your success depends on others and reconnects you to those who supported you during a loss.

Gratitude for people grounds us most deeply. Who are you grateful for today and why? How does gratitude for that person(s) ground you, whether you're soaring or struggling?

I'm Grateful For:

1. ______________________________
2. ______________________________
3. ______________________________
4. ______________________________
5. ______________________________
6. ______________________________
7. ______________________________
8. ______________________________
9. ______________________________
10. ______________________________

Reflections

_/_/_

Signature: ________________

Day 94

A grateful mind doesn't develop overnight. Nothing good does.

Ninety-four days! Not ninety-four breakthroughs—ninety-four days of showing up. Some inspired, some ordinary, and I'm certain some where you wanted to quit. That's grit. You've done the gratitude and I'm certain you've earned peace. All things worth pursuing take time and consistent execution.

What's one thing you've learned about yourself through ninety-four days of consistency? What did showing up, even when you didn't feel like it, teach you?

I'm Grateful For:

1. ______________________
2. ______________________
3. ______________________
4. ______________________
5. ______________________
6. ______________________
7. ______________________
8. ______________________
9. ______________________
10. ______________________

Reflections

_/_/_

Signature: ________________

Day 95

You chose your struggles when you set your goals. They're developing you. Be grateful for them.

"I want to achieve XYZ," is usually said without fully comprehending the obstacles that come with it. If you had all the skills needed to attain that goal, you'd have it. So, your challenges are transforming you into the person who can achieve the goals you set. Imagine attaining your goal without struggling for it—would you trust it? The struggle earns your place.

What is the biggest goal-related challenge you're facing? What happens when you conquer it? What skill(s) are you developing through this experience?

I'm Grateful For:

1. ______________________________
2. ______________________________
3. ______________________________
4. ______________________________
5. ______________________________
6. ______________________________
7. ______________________________
8. ______________________________
9. ______________________________
10. ______________________________

Reflections

_/_/_

Signature: __________________

Day 96

Gratitude is high-octane fuel for growth. But it's a practiced mindset, not a given.

A directed mind has a profound impact on growth. We can't choose which thoughts pop into our minds, but we can choose which ones stay. It's not always easy, but that's when it matters most.

Gratitude is a tool to help you choose. It makes the positive louder and the negative easier to direct away. What thoughts will you allow to incubate in your mind today? Which will you discard?

I'm Grateful For:

1. ______________________
2. ______________________
3. ______________________
4. ______________________
5. ______________________
6. ______________________
7. ______________________
8. ______________________
9. ______________________
10. ______________________

Reflections

_/_/_

Signature: ________________

Day 97

What's not on your gratitude list?

Over 96 days you've examined what you value most in life—the things that keep showing up on your list. But have you noticed what's in your life that doesn't make the list?

Are you overlooking those things, or are you just not grateful for them? If it's the latter, why are they still in your life? How much time are you spending on what you're grateful for versus what you're not? Spend more time on the former. Spend less on the latter—or get rid of it entirely. That's how you move into alignment.

I'm Grateful For:

1. ______________________
2. ______________________
3. ______________________
4. ______________________
5. ______________________
6. ______________________
7. ______________________
8. ______________________
9. ______________________
10. ______________________

Reflections

_/_/_

Signature: ________________

Day 98

The more you're grateful, the less you need.

Over time, gratitude focuses your mind on what matters most. With a daily practice, you begin to notice repeating patterns in your gratitude like relationships or health. By continuously focusing on the blessings in your life, the noise of materialism, envy, and external validation diminishes.

Has your list become repetitive yet? What do you feel most connected to at this point in your journey? Which material goals or external validations have lost their hold on you over these 98 days?

I'm Grateful For:

1. ______________________
2. ______________________
3. ______________________
4. ______________________
5. ______________________
6. ______________________
7. ______________________
8. ______________________
9. ______________________
10. ______________________

Reflections

__/__/__

Signature: ____________________

Day 99

Want everything. Need nothing. Gratitude is the tool.

Reach for the stars and never quit but do so emotionally unattached to the outcome lest you lose your grounding. A grateful mind empowers you to move forward with confidence. Whatever the outcome, it's the one you're meant to have, and there's gratitude in that.

Are you too attached to something right now? List gratitude for your life exactly as it is without that thing. Say, "I want this, but I don't need it. I'm grateful either way." Can you feel the energy shift? If you still observe a hidden feeling of persistent need, that's okay. Letting go isn't a single act; it's a practice, just like gratitude.

I'm Grateful For:

1. ______________________ 6. ______________________

2. ______________________ 7. ______________________

3. ______________________ 8. ______________________

4. ______________________ 9. ______________________

5. ______________________ 10. ______________________

Reflections

_/_/_

Signature: ________________

Day 100

Congratulations! You Fucking Did it!

What you just finished is not for the faint of heart. There's a story in these pages, and you wrote it. A story of 1,000 gratitudes, personal breakthroughs, and days that weren't always easy. You proved you have the discipline and grit required to show up when you don't feel like it. Most importantly, you've shifted your perspective, improved your relationship with life, and earned a new level of peace.

Keep growing, because there is no finish line. The growth you chose for 100 days in a row is the foundation of a life of gratitude and alignment. I hope you're proud of yourself, because I am.

Tomorrow is Day 101. You've earned your peace. Don't lose it. Live in alignment with your values, especially when it's hard, and choose gratitude every day.

I'm Grateful For:

1. ____________________
2. ____________________
3. ____________________
4. ____________________
5. ____________________
6. ____________________
7. ____________________
8. ____________________
9. ____________________
10. ____________________

Reflections

_/_/_

Signature: __________________

THE DAY AFTER

Through 100 days of gratitude and reframing, you embraced the Zero to 54 mindset of taking on challenges, doing what you said you were going to do, and moving forward with gratitude.

That's the same mindset that carried me through a 54-mile ultramarathon having never been a runner. The mindset that empowered me to rebuild a life of alignment after the old one fell apart.

I started this journey searching for fulfillment. That search left me with nothing but response and perspective—the setup I needed to discover what living purposefully actually means. That changed my relationship with life, and I'm confident these 100 days have changed yours too.

But the journal—its format, prompts, aid stations, and accountability—was scaffolding to get you started. The grateful mind you've built doesn't need my guidance anymore. The habit you've built and the values you've revealed are now yours to use.

What will you do with them? What new challenge will you choose that reflects who you are and what you value most?

Go run your mountain.
I love you all.
-Joe

ACKNOWLEDGEMENTS

Walking my journey and writing this book would not have been possible without God and the people who showed up on the hardest days.

The still, small voice: Thank you, God, for never quitting on me, for your unconditional love, for your words, and for being the source of gratitude and all things good.

Nathan, Stella, and Zaina: You are my why. You are why I work so hard to set a good example, why I refuse to quit—especially on the days quitting would be easier, and why the hardest days were filled with so much sunshine. Keep being you, my babies.

Alonzo Cahoon: The only one who witnessed my journey in its entirety. My first real mentor. Thank you for your unwavering belief and handing me the chisel. You saw me when I couldn't see myself and this book would not be possible without you.

Chris Sweis: My best friend. Thank you for always being there and listening to my never-ending loops. Thank you for your wisdom, insights, kindness and love. You are the greatest brother anyone could ever ask for.

Mom and Dad: For giving me my life, a foundation of faith, and your endless love. You set the example of hard work and grit.

Maryann: My "twin." I love you.

The OGs chat, Ronnie Dabbasi, Gary Yaegar, Alex Yousoufian, and Warren Colbert: My guys who always show up. Your presence and friendship mean more than you know.

Anthony Scaramucci: For the handshake, the advice, and always answering. Hopping Over the Rabbit Hole is still your greatest work.

Jonathan Hindi, Monique Walia, Terrie Fontes, and Zoey McClarty: Thank you for your trust, honesty, and contributions. You helped make Part II better for everyone who reads it.

David Haviland: For taking my mess of a manuscript and giving it structure, for teaching me prose, and for telling me things I didn't want to hear but needed to.

Latte Goldstein: For your patience with my endless last-minute edits and overthinking. You took on the design of a 100-day journal when no one wanted to. The book looks fire.

My challenges and my struggles: Thank you for the wisdom, experience, and bringing out my best. Thank you for the opportunity to put my character on display.

Biscuit: You'll never read this but still, you trained me more than I trained you. Thank you for teaching me patience. You're the best dog in the world. I love you.

www.ingramcontent.com/pod-product-compliance
Ingram Content Group UK Ltd.
Pitfield, Milton Keynes, MK11 3LW, UK
UKHW040242300726
14061UKWH00002BD/121